THE COMPLETE
IRON
PALM
By Brian Gray

Disclaimer

Although both Unique Publications and the author(s) of this martial arts book have taken great care to ensure the authenticity of the information and techniques contained herein, we are not responsible, in whole or in part, for any injury which may occur to the reader or readers by reading and/or following the instructions in this publication. We also do not guarantee that the techniques and illustrations described in this book will be safe and effective in a self-defense or training situation. It is understood that there exists a potential for injury when using or demonstrating the techniques herein described. It is essential that before following any of the activities, physical or otherwise, herein described, the reader or readers first should consult his or her physician for advice on whether practicing or using the techniques described in this publication could cause injury, physical or otherwise. Since the physical activities described herein could be too sophisticated in nature for the reader or readers, it is essential a physician be consulted. Also, federal, state or local laws may prohibit the use or possession of weapons described herein. A thorough examination must be made of the federal, state and local laws before the reader or readers attempts to use these weapons in a self-defense situation or otherwise. Neither Unique Publications nor the author(s) of this martial arts book guarantees the legality or the appropriateness of the techniques or weapons herein contained.

ISBN: 0-86568-131-7
Library of Congress Catalog No. 88-51060

Designer: Danilo Silverio
Editor: Dave Cater

UNIQUE
PUBLICATIONS
4201 Vanowen Place
Burbank, CA 91505

Table
of Contents

Foreward

In 1985, I revealed to the readers of *Inside Kung-Fu* magazine the conditioning secrets for iron palm training. My intent was two-fold: to show real iron palm training so those who make fraudulent claims of being masters would find it harder to make a living; and to help those innocent practitioners who sincerely wanted to break solid objects but were sacrificing their hands in the process. I admit I was a little concerned about breaking with tradition in allowing even those *few* secrets to be printed. After a lot of soul-searching and weeks of deep thought, I concluded that such traditional feelings were formed during the times of feudal China, when it was neither wise nor safe to let such secrets fall into the hands of strangers. Times are different now. Feudalism has ended, and I truly would love to see more research done into the incredible feats that are possible with this skill.

Many are impressed with my skills, but I assure you, there are those with skills even greater. When my article was published, the response was incredible. I never knew so many people wanted to know the secrets of the iron palm. I received letters from every country in the world. From the streets of war-torn Beirut, Lebanon, to the mountains of Switzerland, from Canada to Mexico, even from a little town in faraway Malaysia, the letters poured in. And they are still coming. So, I suppose, it should have come as no surprise to me when certain people who want to be known, or simply want to make a fast buck, saw the attention on the subject as a golden opportunity. Suddenly, every master in the world said they had a knowledge of this secret art.

My only question is: Why did these supposed experts wait until now to tell everybody they knew the secret? If they were so concerned about people properly conditioning, where were they in 1973 when I began demonstrating the iron palm? In 1975, I was filmed giving one of my demonstrations at a large martial arts tournament in Washington, D.C. The filming was done without my knowledge, and by a school which, at the time, I did not know. In 1983, the same school told me of the film they had made of my iron palm performance. They also showed me they had copied my movements right down to even the way I stand when I strike the blocks. The film, they told me, had become almost a sacred relic in their school. While I was flattered, I could not help but notice the scarred hands of their instructor. I shared with him the one thing they had not gotten from the film: the necessary steps for proper conditioning. If only he had written, I would have been available to help. It was the sight of his hands that caused me to write that first article in 1985.

I feel, at times, that I inadvertently opened Pandora's Box, but I also feel I must reveal more about the iron palm so the con artists offering their "secrets" will be exposed. I want you to become more educated on the subject so you can identify those who only want to make money, or who would have you believe their martial arts style has had the iron palm all along. Thus, I give you this series on the complete iron palm. Above all, however, I sincerely hope someday to see you impressing me with your iron palm skills.

CHAPTER ONE

History

To thoroughly discuss the iron palm, we must first go back to the beginnings of martial arts history and understand what gave rise to such a deadly skill. The first record of anyone using martial arts is in China in the year 2852 B.C. In one of the old war analects, the Emperor Fu Hsi is recorded to have taught his soldiers organized and defined movements to be used against the enemy. Although the name of this art has changed many times through the centuries, it is now known as kung-fu. It is also known by various names, such as chuan fa, meaning fist art, wushu, meaning martial art, or guo shu, meaning national art. Regardless of the names, one thing remains constant: martial arts has been inextricably interwoven into the fabric of Chinese life through recorded history.

For centuries, China followed the law of feudalism. This rule of might and power meant the strong got stronger and the weak got weaker. For example, suppose you lived in a small village with your mother, father, sister and brother. A band of cutthroats rides into town and decides to rape your sister and mother, before killing them and your father. They then take your brother and you prisoners. You have several options. One is to fight with whatever skills you might possess. The whole village may turn out and fight in an organized fashion, or flee in disunity, leaving you and your family to depend on your resources. If the bandits win, they own your land and village. They can do whatever they want, turning their prisoners into servants. If the bandits lose, the village gains the reputation of being a stronghold, hopefully learning from its battles by organizing town watchmen and even a standing

1

army. The village is safe until someone, or group, stronger than the bandits who failed, tries again.

Sometimes, families would unite for protection. Families with many sons became armies unto themselves, being one of the reasons that daughters were given away in marriage. But sons were expected to stay home and raise families under their parents' roofs. This constant struggle for control of land and power continued over the centuries until warlords owned everything. They, in turn, had families and villages pledged to serve them in return for constant protection. Thus, a warlord's battle strategy was to know the number of villages loyal to any counterpart he was going to attack, as well as to know any special skills the villagers possessed. The poor commoner truly lived by his wits and martial arts skills. Sometimes, it was better to keep his temper and suffer a temporary disgrace, even if he was a good fighter, for beating the wrong man could bring a whole clan down on the head of the unfortunate victor. If one was so skilled to beat a whole clan, it would bring fame and offers to spread his skills. It also meant he would be a target for every would-be fighter wanting to make a name for himself. The unwritten rule was that no one could refuse a challenge. Life was a constant game of chess, with your survival dependent on how fast you could think and react.

Never knowing whom to trust, kung-fu practitioners kept secret their skills, lest their enemies use the same techniques against them. Kung-fu began to be passed down in utmost secrecy, from father to son. Families closely guarded their "secret weapons," (i.e., their special knowledge of fighting). Public demonstrations were not the rule of the wise and prudent. It was safer to either say you knew nothing, or be a powerful warlord who bowed to no one. Many weapons were born out of China's feudalism. They were family secrets, often exposed to the public for the first time when these same families were forced to war. Only when these people had to choose between life or death, did they show their skills. Thus the old Chinese saying: "Beware the fury of a patient man." Battle survivors learned what worked and what didn't. The best techniques were kept, and the rest discarded. The evolution of martial arts in China is more complex than in any other country in the world.

Herbal knowledge also goes back many centuries, and in every province there are secret family recipes for everything from poisons to cures. It is no mystery, then, that eventually someone would use his herbal skills to make the body more impervious to attack. This experimentation eventually led to the advent of the iron palm. By studying herbs and their combinations, a method was discovered to make soldiers impervious to spear thrusts, even without the use of armor. I remember once, years ago, a student of mine, whom I had been training in the iron palm, was horsing around with another classmate before class, and they were attempting a block against a knife. The block was ineffective and my student suffered a knife wound to the palm heel. He was pale as a ghost when his friend brought him to me and related the incident. I sent them to see a doctor, because he was going to need stitches. The doctor straightened two stitching needles trying to pierce my student's hand. He finally had to switch to a heavier gauge needle to pierce the skin and close the wound. So, yes, I believe there was such a thing as "iron vest," where a man could block a spear with his bare body.

These conditioning recipes were closely guarded, which led many to either steal them, or concoct their own. From the many that hoped to duplicate skin, muscle, and bone change, most were worthless. During the Boxer Rebellion, many Chinese died because they had been told by their kung-fu masters that herbal powders and liniments would make them invulnerable to bullets. Many a young martial artist would be informed: "This herbal recipe was handed down to me from the Shaolin Temple itself. This recipe has more ingredients in it than so-and-so's." The Chinese maintain the way to show superiority is to say their particular technique is older, their recipe has more ingredients, or their family tree longer, while reciting endless qualifiers that have **absolutely no relevance**. Thousands of Chinese rubbed useless formulas on their bodies, wore secret charms and amulets, and went through countless rituals only to be misled and eventually killed by the bullet.

It proved to be a sad awakening, yet the Chinese follow much the same principle today. A friend of mine, whose father was a doctor in China, once told me, "If you want to sell a medication in China, you don't say new and improved. You say, instead, very old." Presently, lung cancer accounts for 50 percent of the deaths in China, yet the Chinese people still do not believe there is any correlation between cigarette smoking and the disease. China is a land of mystery to the uninitiated. It can be understood only through a great, great deal of study. China operates within a different system of nature than that to which Americans are accustomed. In America, a history book tells us pretty much what happened. In China, history is clouded, because the accounts were written according to the whims of emperors and empresses whose very frown could cost a man his head. It would not even be safe to speak bluntly after a ruler's death, for the family could rule as a dynasty for centuries. Separating fact from fiction often is impossible.

Many kung-fu masters from China claim to be descended from a long line of kung-fu masters, often tracing their lineage to the Shaolin Temple. Americans are quick to believe these genealogical trees, regardless of whether or not the charts are genuine, or whether or not they have any relevance to the man's skill level. You know, if my father was a successful judge, and his father was a successful judge, and his father, also, I could still be an idiot. That lineage does not guarantee anything. Lineage charts, however, are big business in China, the same could be said for kung-fu. I wish Americans were not so easily duped by false claims. Even the Chinese have a saying that shows they want to see first what a man can do: "Flowering hands, and embroidered legs," referring to flashy performers who may not be able to apply their wild and mysterious movements. The same goes for some of the herbal lotions these men try to sell as necessary for one's training. I know of one herbal lotion, for example, that contains bird feces as one of its ingredients. That is not all. It is to be taken internally. Also, it is still being sold. Those who rush to use any herbal remedy or lotion, just because it was made by a kung-fu master, are no better off than the thousands of Chinese who lost their lives during the Boxer Rebellion because they believed a potion deemed them invincible.

At one point in history, the number of herbal concoctions for skin, muscle, and bone conditioning was numerous. Many of these recipes remain today. Wading through the morass is unnecessary. There are several types of *dit da jow* on the market, and this liniment is all you need for the herbal portion of conditioning. It is the most popular form because it has been proven effective throughout time. Introduced during this time, when everyone was trying to concoct recipes and processes which would produce the iron palm, were methods such as thrusting the hands into sand or working them into heated materials. Many of these were "outer school" methods; that is, they would achieve results, but they lacked the quality found in the "inner school" methods. Such methods as cooking the palm by heating the liniment and workout materials are considered outer school. They leave the hands scarred, reddened and coarse. Disfigurement is unnecessary, and inner school methods promise this will not happen.

We can leave the historical aspect of this discussion with this understanding: because of the intense secrecy necessary to survive

4

centuries of feudalism in China, the secrets of the iron palm were the sole domain of China. Only in the last century has the skill become public knowledge. Chinese call themselves "Center Kingdom People," which came from their ancient beliefs that they were the center of the universe. Everyone else was called a demon. The old Chinese were very ethnocentric, and while an attack from their fellow Chinese was feudally possible, an attack by "foreign devils" was unspeakably intolerable. Therefore, teaching the secrets of kung-fu to foreigners, especially the deeper, deadlier arts, was avoided at all costs. During dynastic downfalls, royal court survivors often exiled themselves in Japan, Korea and Okinawa. While there they gave glimpses of their arts to their host countries, thus leading to the establishment of basic arts in those countries. Nonetheless, skills such as the iron palm were known only to a handful of people, and their secrecy kept it under wraps for centuries.

Conditioning the Palm

Those is considered the superior method of hand conditioning, because it strengthens muscles, skin, and bones, yet leaves no scars, bruises, or deformities. It has been said, and quite erroneously, "The concept is not to make the hand itself harder, but instead to increase striking power by eliminating the pain quotient." This clearly indicates that the person making the statement has not been correctly trained in the iron palm, or he would know the pores of the skin actually draw tighter and form a stronger, denser skin. Also, the muscles and bones are strengthened and can take more stress. For example, when I was unable to train, my hands began to lose their toughness. When I tried to break, I experienced pain; yet when I went back to conditioning, my hand strength and quality returned. It is unquestionable to think the hands do not become harder.

To begin the conditioning process, place in an urn or wok (anything shaped like this will do, such as a pan sled), dried peas at least six inches deep. With the urn on a waist-high pedestal, stand in a horse stance and drop the hand into the peas from shoulder height. Drop the hand 10-to-20 times with the shoulder relaxed, so the shock of impact does not travel back to the heart. If the strike is too tense, the heart suffers. Why only 10-to-20 repetitions? First, it's a progressive thing. A beginner does not need to overdo it, so 10-to-20 is fine. After the hand begins to toughen, the practitioner can decide the number of repetitions. However, 20 repetitions is sufficient.

The hand should be dropped against the striking surfaces you wish to condition, usually the palm, back of the palm and knife edge. Do not strike the fingertips, for this weakens the eyes. Instead, to condition the fingertips, combine fingertip push-ups with raking them back and forth through the pellets. This raking action is performed by pushing forward with the palm heel, then raking back with the fingertips. This helps avoid undue damage to the meridians on the tips of the fingers.

Before and after each session, apply a liberal amount of the Chinese liniment called dit da jow to the hands. Without this liniment, scarring is inevitable. (**Note:** After hearing individuals claim that extra liniments are necessary to the conditioning process and must be used in conjunction with dit da jow, I reiterate that dit da jow is all one needs to properly train. I speak from experience. I have been practicing for decades and have never used anything but dit da jow.) After no less than 10, but no more than 20 strikes with each hand position, stand upright and vigorously shake the hands for a few seconds. This increases the circulation in the hands and allows the blood to help strengthen and change tissue. Next, flex the muscles in the hands by using isometrics, or *chi kung exercises*, which open and close the fists. Push out, then draw back, so the whole arm is worked for circulation. Do this after each set of right and left strikes.

Do not eat for an hour after the workout. You may have something light before starting, but a full stomach will detract from the necessary chemical functions. It is necessary that brain and certain internal organ functions work solely on the area you have brought to their attention — namely, the hands. Also, do not wash the hands for one hour after training. Perform this workout as often as possible. In the Shaolin Temple, it was practiced three times daily: once in the morning, once again at noon, and finally in the evening. To attain the traditional iron palm you must perform this conditioning exercise three times a day for three years. After that, you can train once a week.

After six months, change the peas to an equal mixture of dried peas and stone pebbles. Continue conditioning with this mixture for the next six months; this will complete the first year of training. Entering the second year, discard the dried peas and use only stone pebbles. After six months, mix in an equal amount of iron pellets. The pellets must be of iron (no other metal, not even steel), because iron has properties which mix with the skin. (**Note:** One practitioner told me he was using lead shot. Lead is a poisonous element which is readily absorbed into the skin and can lead to gradual serious destruction of one's health. This explained why the person who called me had been getting ill. I told him at once to stop. Again, **do not** use lead shot.) You should

Instead of striking the pellets with the fingertips, use the method shown here. First push with the palms in a forward direction, then rake back.

(Top photo). A front view of the raking motion from the previous page. The photo above shows the hands of the student after striking the iron pellets and then, after thoroughly applying dit da jow.

Striking the pellets with the knife-edge hand (top). Striking the pellets with the back of the palm (above left). Striking the pellets with the palm (above right).

make sure there are no cuts on the hands during conditioning. This is especially important when one reaches the iron pellet stage; one should not get iron into wounds. However, a more important reason is that some dit da jow recipes are poisonous and can cause death if they enter a wound. Thus, I tell people who do not read Chinese that if they cannot tell whether or not the bottle says "Not for internal use," to always play it safe and keep it out of cuts.

At the two-year mark, discard the pebbles and perform the conditioning exercise using only iron pellets. Continue until you complete the third year of conditioning. At this point, the palm is ready to be used in all iron palm applications and theories. Conditioning is done now only once a day, and eventually, once a week will suffice.

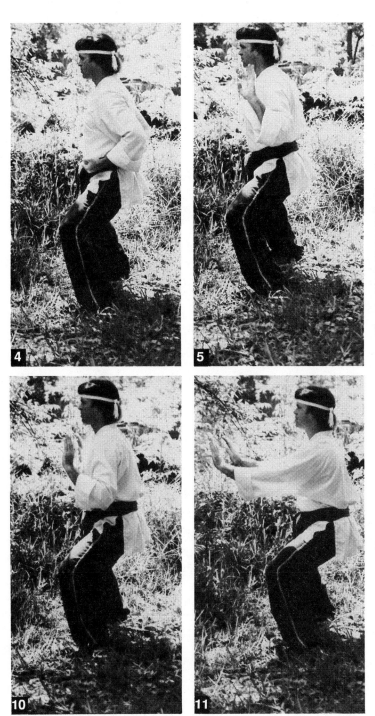

In this series, master Gray shows a chi kung exercise to be performed after iron palm practice. Begin to roll palms down (1). Continue the circle with the palms drawing toward the body (2). Roll the palms over into fists (3). Pull fists back to waist (4). Lift fists, opening into palms as you do so, out to the sides and up to the shoulders (5). Continue the circle, now pushing down to the waist (6). From this position, begin to pull up at the waist (7). Pull up to shoulder height (8). Pull back on the wrists (9). Push forward (10). Return to the first position (11).

CHAPTER THREE

How to Break Solid Objects

Perhaps one of the most impressive aspects of the martial arts is board and brick breaking. In my years of doing appearances and exhibitions, I have never seen it fail. If you want to gain the audience's attention, perform a breaking demonstration. So many people want to perform these feats. They want to impress their friends or scare their enemies. However, few ever realize that the ultimate goal of breaking solid objects is to understand and control one's power.

I once had an idiot come to my school and disparage the skill of breaking boards and bricks. "Why do you break boards and bricks?" he asked, contempt in his voice. "Boards and bricks don't fight back." He was smug when he said this, as though he thought he had me with this little pearl of wisdom; however, I, too, had seen *Enter the Dragon* and knew the famous line delivered by Bruce Lee. I also knew this was not Bruce's intent when he made the statement in the movie. I explained to the idiot (and that is just what he was, a self-taught, self-promoted, pompous idiot who had come to my school with the sole intention of beating me up), that if he had not been taught the reason behind breaking, he was lacking in his education. Board and brick breaking is a slice of the pie, and while it should not be allowed to get out of proportion with the rest of our studies, it is still a slice, without which the pie is incomplete. There are those who learn a few breaking techniques, add some fakery and tricks, and succeed in making a name for themselves. In this chapter, I will show how these frauds do their seemingly spectacular stunts, as well as show the secret to real breaking.

When discussing breaking, we must first begin with the substances you are going to use. Each is treated differently, which many fail to realize. You would be surprised at the people who think if a man can break a board or a brick, he can break anything. They can always be counted on at parties to bring some object up to you and say, "Here, see if you can break this." There are really only three categories a martial artist uses for breaking substances — ice not being one since ice is merely used for sensationalism — and these are wood, brick and stone.

Wood

The most important thing to remember is *grain*. This is the direction in which the fibers of the wood run, and the direction in which planks are cut. When a cross-section is taken from a plank of wood, a practitioner should break the board with the grain, as it will enable him to make

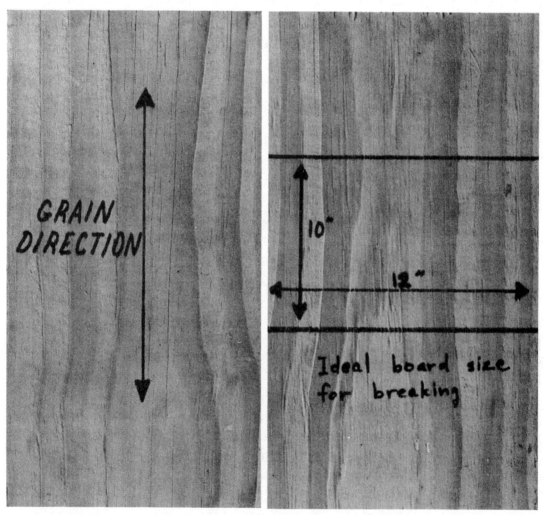

a clean break. Breaking against the grain is more difficult, and, more often than not, results in a splinter break where the board does not completely sever in half.

Naturally, all wood is not the same; therefore, the degree of difficulty in breaking will be determined by several factors: type of tree from which the wood came, thickness of the board, and age of the board. Locust trees are easy to cut when they are green, yet, when their wood has dried and aged, it can destroy the blade of a power saw. At the opposite end of the scale, yellow pine is a soft wood that becomes even easier to break once it has dried. Regardless of the wood, if a knot is present in the center of your board, and if that knot is at least a third of the length of your board, it can make the break impossible. I remember an incident a few years ago when some friends wanted to see me break a stack of nine one-inch boards. It was something I often did, so I nonchalantly walked over to the stack and prepared to break. Try as I might, I couldn't break that particular stack. My friends were beginning to laugh, and with every attempt I made, the laughter grew louder. I kept asking them what was so funny, but they would not tell me. I assumed it was because they doubted my skills and were making fun of me, so I tried all the harder to break that stack. I was going nowhere. When I had had enough, I examined each board. It wasn't until I got to the seventh board that I discovered the problem. That particular board had a knot that traveled its entire length. I won't forget that lesson.

While on the subject of wood, the most popular choice is pine, since it breaks clean, is light and sturdy, and yet is easy to break, which builds a person's confidence. Later, you may use thicker stacks or switch to a more difficult wood such as oak.

Wood thickness is the last thing to consider. Most boards used are called one-inch, yet are purchased in a "finished" state. They have been planed smooth by the manufacturer, and are really only three-quarters of an inch thick. (**Note:** Lumber called "treated" is chemically hardened beyond the wood's normal strength. Often, it will have a greenish color. Do not use this type of wood.) In dealing with thickness, remember that two one-inch boards are easier to break than one two-inch board. A stack composed of any number of boards is always easier to break than a single board equal in thickness to the height of the same stack. It's amazing how few people know this.

Referring back to grain for a moment, I once was doing a demonstration for the March of Dimes, and after it was over, a couple of boys came up to look at some of the items used in the performance. While I was talking to someone else, I watched these guys out of the corner of my eye. What followed was slapstick comedy. They had been impressed by some of my board breaking, and apparently were wondering if they too could do it. So, while one was going to hold the board with both hands, the other boy was going to hit it with his fist as hard as he could., He pulled his fist way back, wound up, and let go. Crack! I would have loved to photograph that boy's face. It was filled with intense pain and the urge to scream (by the way his mouth opened up). The board remained unbroken, while his hand was numb. What these two, who were now looking at me as if I were Superman, did not know were breaking basics. The boy attempting to break was not trying one of my boards in its unused state. He had, instead, a remnant from an earlier break. Suppose the board that I had broken measured 12 inches by 10 inches. What these boys had was a board 12 inches by 5 inches, looking more like a short section of bed-slat. Even *I* would not have tried to break that board. Making it all the more difficult was that one boy was holding the board. By not placing it on a stable, moving support, the thickness of the board dramatically increased. A board only one-inch thick can become the same as one three, or four inches thick. If you cannot break a three-inch board, you are not going to break that one-inch board until it is stabilized.

Brick

In this category we include every type of brick, or block, manufactured. If it is man-made, it falls into this category. Knowledge of brick manufacturing processes has helped many a fraud hide his lack of talent. Every brick has at least two basic elements — a raw material and a binder. The raw material is what the brick is made of, such as sand, clay, or crushed stone. The binder is the chemical used to cause the raw material to "set up" or harden. Sometimes extra ingredients are added to make the brick even stronger. Centuries ago, early settlers added such things as horse hair and straw to their clay bricks. Today, elements such as granite chips are added. **Note:** *It is virtually impossible to tell what is inside that brick by simple observing its outside.* Why is this so important? Because, you may be breaking an ordinary brick, and get to feeling pretty good about yourself. You start to think all bricks similar to those you've been breaking are easy to break. You grab a convenient brick to show some friends your martial prowess, and, *voila,* you hurt your hand, not the brick. Knowing the composition of a brick is a must.

This reminds me of a story in which an American was studying in China and came across a public kung-fu demonstration. The school's senior student was giving a breaking exhibition and broke a brick with ease. After the audience applauded, he produced a similar brick and offered a member of the crowd the chance to duplicate his feat. The American caught his eye, and to impress the foreigner with the Chinese skill level, he convinced the American to try. Everyone was laughing at his effort to accomplish what had come easy to the kung-fu student. Swift thinking, though, saved the day. The American asked the Chinese student if he could break it. He could *not!* Why? Because the student had made the bricks himself, and in the center of the one he gave the American, he had placed an iron bar.

Before trying to break any type of brick, you should obtain a sample of the bricks to be used and break it in half by using a hammer. Then, look at the contents and note its composition. If you see what appears to be rock chips, then it is aggregate and harder to break than one without chips. Sometimes it is impossible to tell by looking inside. Do not be fooled by appearances. Another method of making a brick harder is to use finer sand and vibrate the mixture. The only way to tell the difference is to place one that had not been vibrated next to one that had. With practice, you will learn to notice the very fine ripple effect it gives the outer surface of the brick. Still, to the untrained eye the two blocks will appear the same. Another method for making the block harder is the ratio of cement to sand; the more sand, the weaker the block, the more cement, the stronger the block.

At the beginning and end of a run (the process of making the bricks), the bricks have more sand than cement. They may look the same but the first and last ones will be weaker.

I once found several Korean "grandmasters" going to a particular blockmaker and requesting the blocks from the beginning and end of the runs. They were buying all the soft blocks and using them for their public demonstrations. I personally went to the manufacturer to ask him if it was true that he made "master" so-and-so's blocks. He replied that he did, and I then asked him what was unusual about this particular block. He said, "Well, they are from the beginning of the run, so they're about 90 percent sand, and we don't let them set up (hardening process). My little 4-year-old could sit on them and they'd fall apart." These people who were making the blocks for these quasi-masters were unaware that they were being used to dupe the public. When I asked them why these masters needed to buy weak blocks for breaking, he replied, "Oh, well, they say they are for their students so they won't hurt their hands." I laughed and said, "Well, then, when do these masters come and buy their blocks?" From then on, the manufacturer refused to sell these frauds any more weak blocks.

Another way bricks and blocks will vary in strength is the raw material itself. Cinder is weak, and any self-respecting martial artist will refrain from using it. Clay and sand are next in strength, and the hardest are made from crushed stone or marble. I will never forget how I learned about crushed marble. It was 1973, and I would usually go over to the place where I bought my blocks and practice breaking techniques in their stockyard. After I was finished, I would go inside and pay my bill. A nice arrangement, because I didn't have to carry them home. Sometimes they could even resell the halves. We were both happy. On this particular day, one of the men who worked there said he had a brick he wanted me to break. I agreed to try. It looked so easy, I was amazed he wanted me to break it. After all, the bricks which I customarily broke there were much bigger, so I could not conceive of this block being a challenge. It was only one inch thick, by four inches wide, by 16 inches long. "A piece of cake," I thought. But when I struck it, I did not even make a dent! I tried every technique I knew. Still nothing. After I was thoroughly convinced that no one was going to break that brick with his bare hands, I slammed it against another piece of brick to open it up. I just had to see the inside of this brick. The fact that the outside of the brick was white and smooth as polished glass was at first no cause of concern, but when I saw the inside was all white and sparkling, I asked the composition of the block. "Marble," he replied. But that still did not justify it being impossible to break. After all, marble is hard, but this brick was long and thin. It should have broken. On further questioning, I found that it was not only marble, but marble powder. This marble powder was very fine, and been vibrated down, and had been allowed to "set up" for seven years! Setting up, or aging, makes a brick harder; however, this is only when the aging is done under proper drying conditions.

There is an exception to every rule. Some types of aging actually weaken a brick. If a brick has been buried underground, such as in the foundation of a home, the constant contact with the ground and the elements will tend to leech the brick of its strength. Also, extreme heat conditions, such as bricks used to line a fireplace, will weaken them with time. Bricks that have been subjected to these conditions are more brittle, and, therefore, will snap with less pressure. Many frauds know this and will bake bricks prior to their exhibitions. If you want to see the fraud embarrassed, wait until they are doing some great breaking feat, such as breaking four or five bricks with a knife-edge hand, and then hand them a nice, new brick that came straight from the factory and contains little aggregate. Unless he knows some of the phony breaking techniques, the break will be unsuccessful. And that after just having shown his ability to break several with one blow. The tipoff was the use of substandard-looking bricks. I am always just a little skeptical when I see a breaking demo done with old-looking bricks. If they want to impress me, they will have to use *new* bricks.

Stone

This is the most difficult and unpredictable substance to break. As any geologist will tell you, you can grade the hardness of a particular stone by knowing the family of minerals from which it comes. Whether a stone is jade or quartz, obsidian or sandstone, the hardness will be on a scale of 1-to-10, with a diamond being 10. No two stones are going to be the same because of flaws inherent in each stone. You can take two stones of equal size and shape, yet one will contain a flaw and therefore be easier to break. There is no way to standardize breaking when dealing with stones; breaking stone makes one believe masters may merely be exploiting the knowledge of a stone's weakness at the expense of his audience.

Arsenal of weapons

We next come to hand and foot positions. There are both good and bad anatomical weapons; the only difference being what one is willing to sacrifice for a lethal weapon. Some people feel that a deformed hand is all right; I disagree. I recommend against bone contact for breaking. The best weapons are those which use muscle tissue over bone, such as the knife-edge hand, palm heel, and hammerfist. For kicking, the best techniques use the bottom of the heel, and the foot in a knife-edge position. Use of the bone contacting parts can cause unsightly and sometimes permanent damage. This is unnecessary because just as much can be achieved without destroying the hands or feet.

The best analogy I can give to compare weapon types is that of the difference between a wooden mallet or hammer and one made of rubber. If you strike a brick with the wooden mallet, the brick will break with less effort than if you strike it with the rubber one. Yet,

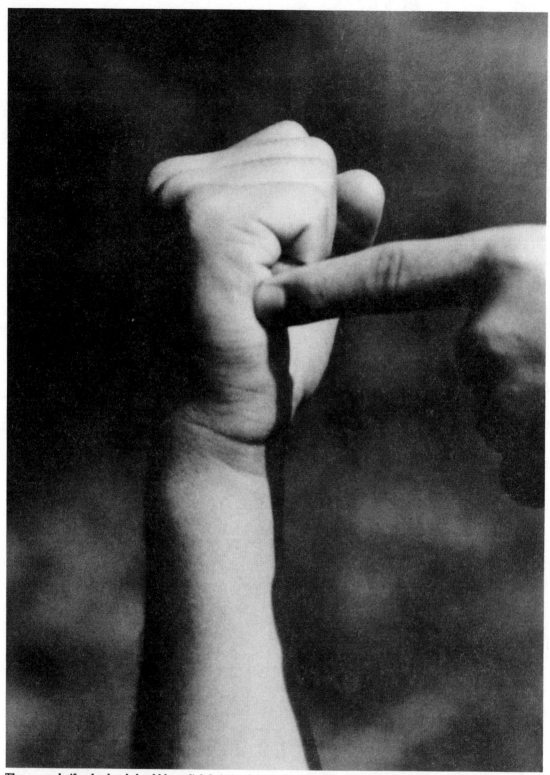

The proper knife-edge hand should lean slightly inward, away from the bones. Avoid hitting the wrist or fingers.

it must be remembered it is possible to break the brick with the rubber one. Many people feel that to break a brick they must use their knuckles to form a harder contact surface. When you have learned to use the iron palm, you will feel sorry for those who have deformed their hands by pulverizing their knuckles. The palm can go through just as much as the knuckle-exposed fist.

After having chosen the material as well as the hand or foot position, all that remains is the actual theory of breaking. This is where so many get into trouble, because they were self-taught, or worse, taught by someone who was self-taught. I say worse, because at least the former can be corrected by showing them the error of their ways, but the latter have been brainwashed into loyalty to a blind man. They may not listen to you long enough to discover their mistakes.

In discussing the actual breaking theory, there are five principles to remember: breathing, focus, concentration, speed, and aim. They are important, individually and collectively, and will make the difference between success or failure in every attempt.

First in our discussion is understanding the importance of breathing. Always remember to breathe *out* when executing the break. When I was taught how to break, I remember being told to breathe out from the bottom of the lungs. I thought this was a strange request. "How does one breathe from the bottom of the lungs?" To understand the answer, exhale until all air is out of your lungs. You will find you can make one last, very small, exhalation. This causes a tightening of the muscles, which further aids your breaking, and is the exact moment when proper breaking is done. In other words, your break should be executed near the point where you reach the last forced exhalation. The "kiai" used by many Japanese stylists is an example of this principle. The long, drawn out "ki. . ." is the exhalation, the final ". . .ai" is the moment of striking. Next is our discussion of focus. If you turned and walked into a glass door you did not know was there, you would hit it harder than at any other time, because your attention was focused beyond the door. If, on the other hand, you were told to repeat that same performance, you would pull back each time because you feared hurting yourself. When you were focused beyond that door, there was no hesitation. This example has a direct correlation to breaking theory. When breaking, the focus must go beyond the object to be broken. There can be *no* hesitation. The mind must be convinced the goal of the hand or foot is beyond the board or brick, and the object to be

Beginning students often center their palms to look visually centered (1). However, turning the palm over and pointing to the center of the palm helps see that the palm was not at true center (2).

broken does not lie in the path of the goal. Focus beyond the object being struck, forgetting it exists altogether.

Being hesitant is important in more ways than one. Besides disrupting your force, it also adversely affects your speed and concentration. When you hesitate, and keep yourself from successfully breaking the board or brick, you make your hand hurt a little more and a little more, until, finally, with each unsuccessful hit, you begin to fear striking the board or brick because the pain gradually worsens. It is a self-defeating cycle seen so many times in beginners who are conquered by their fears. Your focus must go beyond your fears.

Concentration is third in our discussion. You cannot be distracted when you attempt to break. Your concentration should only be on what you are doing. You must mentally review the ingredients to a proper break. As you advance in breaking skill, it will take less and less time to make this mental review. A master will break without thinking. He does not think, he merely does.

Speed is an essential breaking ingredient. The faster your hand or foot moves, the more kinetic energy is stored. At the moment of impact,

You can see (1) where the improperly centered palm would have been striking. Master Gray demonstrates (2) proper centering of the palm.

that speed must be translated, or changed, into something else. It is the manner in which it is translated or changed that results in the various levels of breaking techniques. You must remember that any hesitation during the execution of the strike changes the amount of stored kinetic energy. In other words, the potential breaking power in the hand or foot can be drastically reduced if hesitation is introduced into the technique. Fear cannot exist. Speed can be achieved through several techniques. The one beginners use is simple muscle contraction; the more muscle they have, the harder and faster they swing the hand. In the application of internal techniques, there is another method which generates speed of a more intense nature, and that is the "wave."

In describing this technique, one should think of how a wave of water moves. Water is so pliable you cannot grasp it with your hands. Place your hand in water, grab a handful and bring it to you. What have you got? Nothing. Yet, stand in its way and you will immediately feel its force. What made that soft, pliable water feel like a brick wall? It is the gathered momentum. Thus, to apply this lesson to striking, think of a wave that begins at the foot, travels up the leg past the knee, past the thigh, is amplified in the hips, continues on up the back to the shoulders, and goes out and down the arms to reach, finally, the hand. Make this a non-broken, non-stop wave of motion. It must feel like a whip has been cracked. This force augmentation can be incredible.

A good analogy is the cracking of a bullwhip. Most people don't know what makes the cracking sound when a whip is snapped. The hand begins a wave by moving up, then rapidly down. This wave is translated into the whip itself, which finds it must convert all the kinetic energy of a hand that is bigger than the whip is thick, and whose arc (the distance between the highest and lowest points in the swing of the hand), cannot be matched by the upward and downward movement of the whip, because the whip was at the same time pulled in a backward direction, thus forcing the wave that has been formed to be put into forward motion. The whip cannot move up and down far enough, because the wave's forward motion will not give it time. This causes the upward and downward motion to be less than the hand's; therefore, the lost distance is converted into forward speed. By the time the wave has raced to the end, it is forced into the still smaller thickness of the whip's tip. It must convert the loss of thickness in the whip, and the loss of height in the initiating swing, into an equal expenditure of energy which comes out in the form of speed. The loud "crack" that you hear when the whip is cracked is a miniature sonic boom. The tip of that whip is doing more than 600 miles per hour! Now think about it. How fast was your hand going? To be sure, it wasn't 600 miles per hour, nor anywhere near that speed. As you can see, a wave can change things.

Finally, we come to aim, the fifth principle of a successful break. It seems so simple that one would be quick to dismiss it and say, "C'mon, everybody knows they've got to aim." This is, however, where the real mystery comes into play. I say mystery because so many people do everything else right, but still can't figure out why they are unsuccessful. Many students have looked at me after failing a break, and invariably given me that same "What did I do wrong?" look. They did everything right — except aim. They began by aiming, but while they were attempting the break, something threw them off course.

First, there are those, who in the excitement and energy of the moment, do not realize they are closing their eyes as they strike, and thus, are not looking at the target. Hundreds fail for this reason alone. Another reason for failure is to miss the center of the target.

When I teach a student the iron palm, I have him place his palm on top of the block he is going to break. He almost always places the palm to appear visually centered, measuring from the wrist to the fingertips. Yet this is not correct. Then I have him turn his palm over and place the back of the hand on the block. I ask him to place the tip of the finger of his free hand on the center of his open palm, the palm heart, and note the point. That is true center for a palm slap, the center of the palm, yet, when he looks at how he had centered the palm before, he finds he was actually off center. He was actually nearer to one-third of the way in, instead of halfway, or center. The closer you come to the edge, the harder the object will be to break. Aim is crucial. While you may think you are hitting the same object, an improper aim will make it respond as though its thickness has increased.

Fraudulent Breaking Methods

I sincerely hope that after reading this section on frauds and their breaking techniques, you will never be among the suckers who have had the wool pulled over their eyes. There are thousands of charlatans out there who pass themselves off as the real thing, yet are all merely hiding behind a display of breaking skill that amounts to nothing more than cheap tricks and showmanship. Remember: any person can break a solid object. Breaking solid objects does not make one a martial arts expert. It merely makes one a breaker of solid objects. A slice of the pie is still just a slice of the pie. An expert martial artist knows how to break solid objects, because that has been part of his total training. Remember this when seeing a breaking demonstration: Many automatically assume that the performer is legitimate, and that he knows a complete martial arts system; however, if he is phony enough to pull fraudulent breaking stunts, he is phony enough to call himself an instructor, master, or whatever he needs to take your money. A man must demonstrate a lot more than just breaking to qualify as a martial arts expert.

The most popular trick is spacers. This is used even by people who are qualified martial artists and who ought to have enough integrity to leave it alone. Anytime someone places a spacer between something to be broken, he is trying to impress the audience, plain and simple. He is creating the illusion of breaking more than he really can. If someone says it is not so, ask him to remove the spacers and complete the performance. He can't do it. Why? Because breaking with spacers is simply a matter of keeping the momentum going after the first board snaps. Break the first board and the momentum does the rest. If the spacers are far enough apart, then the break practically works itself. Sometimes people will use too thin spacers, hit the stack too slow, or with not enough power, and they will end up breaking only a portion of the stack on the first hit. No matter what the person is breaking, if spacers are used, he only is breaking the top board or brick.

A discussion of spacers brings us to another sensational trick — ice breaking. A rule to remember is that ice expands when it freezes and contracts when it thaws. So when someone is going to break a large block of ice, the longer they have to wait the harder the feat will be. This must have been the reason why theatrical types — those who break the large stacks of ice — resorted to a practice known as "scoring" the ice. It is already bad enough that they are using huge spacers. Take a look at those pictures of famous ice breakers. Notice they all use spacers. What keeps the break going is the weight of each block crashing onto the one below. But each of those blocks has been "scored," that is, they used a saw to cut three-to-four-inch deep grooves into the tops and bottoms of the ice. The ice has been weakened and is easier to break. A legitimate ice breaker will let the ice be stacked one block on top of the other, with no spacers and or score marks.

Another fraudulent, albeit impressive technique, involves holding two bricks in one hand and shearing them in half with a knife-edge hand. It seems so amazing, people fail to see reality staring them in the face. Although the bricks appear to be held in an ordinary grip, they are really leaning slightly apart with the aid of one of the fingers, usually the index finger. The bricks are thereby spaced, imperceptibly so to the audience, but only a small amount of space is needed for this trick. The expert merely smacks the two bricks together hard enough and the rest takes care of itself. The way to expose these frauds is to insist they repeat that same feat with only *one* block, reasoning that, if they could do two, surely they could do one. They won't be able to break just one, because there is nothing against which to smack the brick. They'll give you plenty of excuses as to why they can't do it, but any refusal will be hard to justify. If you know there won't be enough bricks left after the demo, insist the two bricks be tightly taped so spacing is impossible. You will stop the fraud in his tracks.

Another trick using the same principle involves the expert laying a brick on top of a support brick. While down holding the brick with one hand, he slices off the end of the brick with his other hand. I have seen this done with one or more bricks. The trick is done this way:

One of the more awe-inspiring breaking techniques at demonstrations involves holding two bricks with one hand (above left) and shearing them in half with a knife-edge hand. While impressive, it's not true breaking magic. As you can see by the photograph, the bricks are being held slightly apart—or spaced so that when the bricks strike each other, they break. Another fantastic breaking feat, which is more sleight-of-hand than true technique, is slicing off one end of the brick with one hand (above right). Although the brick to be broken appears to be held flat against a hard surface, one end is really angled up. As the knife-edge hand comes down on the brick, the hand maintaining the grip simultaneously releases and the object is slammed against the brick on which it is resting. This causes a quick break.

The brick to be broken seemingly is held down with one hand, while the other hand shears off the part of the brick hanging over the edge. Yet the brick being held down actually is being held *up*. The fingers hold the block up by just using the palm. As the knife-edge hand comes down on the brick, the hand maintaining the grip simultaneously releases and the object is slammed against the brick on which it is resting. This causes a quick break. This would be a great trick if you wanted to scare someone, because you can break any size brick with this method. To catch the fraud here, do not stare at the break, but rather at the space under the brick to be broken. That brick should be tightly against the support block the *entire* time. There is *no* excuse for *ever* lifting it.

By using a little imagination and innovation, along with special hand positions, the list of fraudulent techniques greatly increases. One time, when I was about to perform for a special grand opening, a man told me that he could break my blocks with one finger. I knew my blocks could not be broken by his one finger, because they were concrete and too thick for his unconditioned hands. I very politely told him I would be interested in someday seeing the trick, and then excused myself.

I learned later his supposed one-finger technique was a sham, which came as no surprise. This was his plan: He would make a fist and brace the index finger against the thumb, making it look as though he was going to hit with the extended finger. But actually, it was the side of his fist doing the breaking. With the right speed, no one noticed, and he fooled a lot of people. Now couple that technique with breaking two bricks held in one hand and you can imagine how impressed a crowd could be.

One should not forget how a photograph can enhance the reputation of many breaking frauds. Many a phenomenal-looking picture has been staged. While it is often necessary for legitimate experts to stage their photos, knowledge of how to set up these shots opens the door to fraudulent practice. Here are two of the more obvious frauds' techniques. One has the expert hitting the block with the photo showing the hand at the moment of impact. One only has to look closely to see that the "expert" is using a palm heel strike, not a palm slap. The iron palm is just that, a palm not a palm heel. By using the heel of the palm, you are employing the bones of the arm, as well as muscle, whereas, the true iron palm uses only the center of the palm known as the palm heart. Using the palm heel strike does not give that practitioner the right to say he has the iron palm. The palm heel strike is external, while the iron palm slap is internal. The other example actually is a series of photographs. One sequence showed the hand about to strike, the hand going through the object, and the hand resting over the broken object. The caption made us think this was the Korean version of the Chinese iron palm, noting the hand in the final photo was in a *palm* position. At first glance, you assume the Korean was a true iron palm practitioner, because you could clearly see he was going through the object and finishing in a palm slap position. Yet, by taking a closer look at the second photo, you would see the Korean was actually using a *knife-edge* hand strike. Why did he pose with his palm instead of his knife-edge hand in the final photo? Because the photos, article and accompanying headline were purposely misleading and misrepresenting. In my book, that constitutes fraud.

While discussing photos, I should remind you that sometimes a martial artist will write an article, and will have no photos to submit. Editors will often use other photos to go with the article. While it is not the intent of the magazine or its editors to mislead the public, readers often mistakenly think the photo accompanying the article is that of the author. I noticed one photo did not show the performer's face, only his hand and the bricks being broken. However, I recognized the photo as one used years ago on the cover of a martial arts magazine. The man in that picture was not Chinese, although the author of this particular article was. The illusion, though, was that this author not only was writing about the iron palm, but showing his skill in the close-up photo. This type of accidental endorsement by the magazine gave legitimacy to the author even though the information in the article was wrong. People often ask why my information differs from other supposed iron palm masters. Anyone can write anything, but if a man claims to have the iron palm, I want proof in one of two ways: Either I see him perform a verifiable iron *palm* break, or I see him perform the same on film, showing that none of the blocks were soft, cracked, or tampered with in any manner.

The trouble with the average martial arts enthusiast is that he is ready to believe anyone who claims to have the iron palm. Some of the garbage I see peddled as advice on how to practice and learn this ancient art is so unfounded and wrong I often wonder how people can be so gullible. As the knowledge of the iron palm becomes more widespread, more and more people are going to claim expertise. When karate was introduced here, it wasn't long before frauds appeared. They neither considered how hard the true experts worked to attain their skills, nor afforded them the proper respect. These frauds gave themselves incredible titles and credentials. When the ninja craze hit, the same thing happened. In almost every city in America, you can find some swift operator passing himself off as a ninja master. The old advertising slogan, "The quality goes in before the name goes on," is so useful here.

A master at the Shaolin Temple was a man who had spent 15-to-20 years training. I have seen guys, who got pretty good at tournament sparring, call themselves master after only *three* years. I knew opening the doors to the secrets of the iron palm would be inviting trouble, but it was the only way to help the public spot frauds. You must do your homework. There's no place for laziness in the life of a true martial artist. Learn your art, know how the frauds operate, and speak out when you see injustice. I know of no greater sin than silence in the face of injustice.

CHAPTER FIVE

Striking With the Iron Palm

Whenever I perform in public, a million questions follow. Some ask, "Does it hurt your hand?" Others inquire, "How do you do that?" "Is it mostly in your mind?" Any type of breaking will only be successful if the basics have been mastered. That is step one. However, beyond ordinary breaking there are levels which require meditation and constant conditioning. Without the meditation, the forces necessary for the higher levels of breaking cannot emerge, and without constant conditioning, the hands will lose the strength needed to handle the extra stress.

The best way to answer the most-often asked questions is to describe the steps as I go along. It's easy to break one slab of concrete, so, short of taking it for granted, I do not exert all my potential. There is no need to destroy the slab, just break it, and with the power I possess, I know I will shatter the slab if I hit it will full power. So, the first thing I do is tone down my effort. Toning down too much, however, has resulted in being unable to break a two-inch thick slab of concrete on the first try. Yet, right after that demonstration, I'd break six inches on the first attempt. Only through constant practice will you know how much effort is needed.

After determining how much force I need to break the slab, and taking aim to break on the exhale, I am ready to bring up the force that flows through the palm and does the breaking. To prepare to break on the exhale, I lift my palm off the slab as I inhale, and slowly exhale and lower the palm back onto the slab. I raise and lower my palm

Master Gray demonstrates the correct wave motion of the palm in this series of photos.

The height of the wave depends on the thickness and strength of the object to be broken, but should go no higher than the shoulder.

By now, the force is pulling down on the elbow, then the wrist, and finally the palm.

At this point, make sure the thumb is tucked firmly alongside the index finger. This prevents the side of the thumb joint from being damaged.

Keep the feet clear of the break. Often, the impact of master Gray's palm will cause the support blocks to be knocked over as well.

with a waving motion to prepare for the actual application of the palm to the slab. As I mentioned earlier, I was filmed by a martial arts school during an iron palm demonstration in Washington, D.C., in 1975. I did not find out I had been filmed until 1983, when I returned to Washington, D.C. I discovered they had been analyzing that film all those years, hoping to learn my secrets. They erroneously believed my skill came from the way I hit, so they never conditioned their hands. They paid a dear price for their ignorance. However, they had memorized the motion I make with my palm. I like my palm to hit the concrete surface just as my exhalation hits its apex.

The final act is to create the force that makes the break possible. Starting with the toe, I visualize a wave that begins with physically rocking the body back on the ankle, while keeping the foot firmly planted. This motion resembles the back-and-forth cracking of a whip, traveling from the toe to the leg, leg to the hips, hips to the back, back to the arms, and down and out through the palm. This path is one continuous whip, and the mind should sense an unbroken line of motion traveling from the initiating to the terminating point.

Bear in mind that while I am using my palm, I am observing the rules for breaking that I earlier outlined. However, I have been using the iron palm for so long, I do it as a matter of course. I am really only aware of exhaling, making the wave, and channeling meditative powers that enhance my internal strength. There is a misconception that comes from watching an iron palm demonstration. Many people will remark that I appear to be gently hitting the slab of concrete when I break. They conclude that they must break with a soft slap. This is wrong. The motion only appears gentle. A powerful muscular contraction occurs during the break.

It is impossible to flex the palm and not flex the muscles of the arm, so when I slap concrete at high speed, the action is over before I can even begin to relax the arm. I discuss this point because there are some who say that only the palm should be flexed at the moment of impact. It is a physical impossibility; unless you fling your hand and arm like snapping a wet towel, you must flex the muscles of the palm to properly place the palm in its striking position. In doing so, you flex the pectoral muscles which are over the heart. This transmits a certain amount of shock back to your heart, and I find the harder you hit, the more of a thump your heart feels. Therein lies the danger for those who improperly train. Flexing must follow the wave of motion.

In other words, imagine the flexing going away from the heart and down the arm to the flattened palm. This keeps the shock wave, generated by the energy exchange at the point of contact, from coming back up the arm and hitting you in the chest. I have felt this, and it *burns*. I was breaking six inches of concrete for an exhibition. When I hit that stack, I simultaneously flexed the whole arm. This is a lot like taking a baseball bat and letting the end drop. If you drop the end with a wave of motion flowing down your arm and through the bat, your hand will feel next to nothing. But interrupt the wave and notice the kick when the bat hits. The danger lies in giving your heart a jolt when the palm is improperly applied to such a large quantity of concrete. It takes so much power to break this large quantity, you do not want it coming back. Not only is this bad on your heart, I never again want to feel that awful burning sensation in my heart. Repeatedly abusing your heart in this manner can lead to a heart attack.

After breaking one slab of two-inch thick concrete, the next step is two at once. Once I add that extra slab, I dispense with gentle slaps. Four inches is a lot of concrete, especially since I use concrete with granite chips. Now I have to hit harder, but later we shift gears and use other factors. Hitting harder is like turning up the volume. The same goes, for the most part, when I do three or more slabs, except when I reach this point, I add the "meditative factor," which also will be explained later. When you plan to break the entire stack, you have to increase the effort. However, when you reach a point where increasing the effort is not enough, the meditative factor comes into play. Although this factor may vary from person to person, I find one most effective. At the end of one of my iron palm videos is footage from a television appearance. The host of the show says, "Watch now as master Gray attempts to break only the bottom brick." In front of the whole world (I found this segment even aired in Taiwan), I broke the entire stack, instead of just the bottom block. I said, "Sorry," as I walked away. I guess the producers thought that was cute (they left that part in), but my original intent was to show one of the internal breaking skills, so I was disappointed in the outcome. However, making the break too powerful was the meditative factor. Here is how it happened:

The television cameramen were all set to film. An air of tenseness permeated the school. My students were not used to being filmed for television and the television people were not used to being in a kung-fu school. Our school resembled a temple — lanterns burning, incense filling the air, uniforms and weapons — and the camera crew was in awe. Never having been before the television cameras, my students were afraid they were going to trip and destroy something expensive. Camera crew and kung-fu student alike moved with undue ceremony and stiffness. I had to keep trying to set everyone into a more relaxed frame of mind and still concentrate on what I was doing. When we finally came to my last iron palm demonstration, we stacked four inches of paper on top of two-inch concrete slabs. I was demonstrating my ability to go through the paper, through the first two slabs and break only the last block.

The camera crew positioned lights only a few feet away. While not visible to the television audience, they were very close and very intense. When I say intense, I still saw light, literally, when I closed my eyes. My concentration broken, I did not break the block as intended on my first strike. Right then, I had to make a split-second decision. Should I continue to slap with the amount of concentration that I was using, or should I use the meditative factor? If I continued and needed two or three more hits, the cameras would roll and my mistakes would air. I wanted to break it on the next hit, yet my concentration was being destroyed by a combination of that intense light, knowing I had already hit it once and failed, and realizing the cameras had *not* stopped rolling. They were filming my every move. They were filming every second I took.

Where was I during that split-second when I was making up my mind? What was I doing? I saw myself in the courtyard of the Shaolin Temple. I visualized it so well, that I could see the banners of the temple fluttering in the breeze over the rooftops, and could smell the scent of the pine trees swaying gently nearby. The sky was blue, and white clouds floated overhead. The noonday sun felt warm on my forehead, and I knew the masters soon would want me to show them my iron palm training. When class convened, they would want a demonstration so they could mark my progress. Right now, though, I was alone in the temple grounds, no pressure, no audience. It felt so good to be a part of the famous Shaolin Temple. The honor, the discipline, the integrity, the intensity! I felt like I was standing in the middle of a giant power plant, its electricity flowing along the routes of my muscles. I felt a literal tingling as my galvanic skin response prickled. Physically, I was at my kung-fu school; mentally, I was centuries and thousands of miles away.

When I opened my eyes, I was still at the Shaolin Temple. I no longer noticed the light. I also forgot I was going to break *only* the bottom block. I only remembered I had to break the block beneath my hand. When you watch the video, look at the difference in my facial expression when they showed me at the moment before my first attempt, the moment my face re-enters the screen, and the moment I broke all six inches. It was a different me who went through that whole stack. Going back to the Shaolin Temple and drawing on that internal power took just enough time to raise my hand a second time, yet the two attempts were worlds apart.

Have you ever seen something so impressive it gave you goosebumps? This is how I describe the meditative factor to laymen. A memory that elicits goosebumps with each recall is a key to an inner power we all possess. Draw on that memory. Be it a sight, a sound, an experience, it must be so intense that it causes your very skin to prickle. Learn to call this up at will and focus it on your breaking technique. It will open many doors for you.

Finally, we come to the question on the minds of most potential breakers: How to choose which blocks in a stack are to be broken? First, you must exercise patience or you will never master this skill, which is the most time-consuming of all iron palm techniques.

The secret is to think "depth." Sounds simple, but it takes constant breaking practice to achieve proper depth, strike the stack, and release just enough force with the right kind of continuum behind it. Depth and making your force explode at contact is directly related to the amount of contact your palm makes with the concrete surface. The greater the depth, the longer the palm remains in contact with the concrete, yet to break only certain blocks in the stack, the palm must quickly come off of the stack. This is different from breaking the entire stack, where the palm goes to the other side of the stack. In other words, when breaking a whole stack, the palm remains in constant contact with the stack; when selectively breaking, the palm must instantly come off the stack. With years of practice, you will learn how to set the depth. Patience, patience, patience. There are no tricks, so prepare to work long and hard.

You now know how to learn, practice, and master this rare and deadly art. I realize there still might be questions. When I wrote about the conditioning method several years ago, mail came pouring in from all over the world. I saw that I had engendered more questions than I had answered. Hundreds of letters, thousands of questions. and I personally answered them all. I am flattered by all the attention, but my ultimate goal is for others to build on this knowledge. I want someday to see someone give *me* goosebumps by performing the iron palm.

Beware of "masters" who cloak their inabilities in secrecy. Do not be conned by those who are only out to sell you something, yet cannot prove they have the genuine iron palm. If you have not seen a demonstration with your own eyes, be slow to believe. Since I wrote my first article, I have seen plenty of merchants set up shop. I am not referring to honest masters receiving justified remuneration for their skills; rather my complaints lie with those who became "instant" masters following my 1985 article. I remember when my friends would train to win in tournaments, while I would spend my time in the quarries slapping stones or in the supply yards breaking concrete blocks. I remember how alone I was, how much of an "oddity" I seemed to be even to my fellow martial artists. Now, suddenly, I see iron palm masters coming out of the woodwork. They are everywhere, even from countries that used to call the Chinese iron palm the "Chinese fantasy." Be on the lookout for frauds. There are only a handful of genuine iron palm masters in the world. Many people ask me where they can find a master in this city or that. I am amazed at how easy they think they can find one. They cannot be found on every street corner. I hope this book will keep you from being suckered by the frauds among us.

Also, I hope I have made the art a little more accessible to everyone, and that it will be used to uphold justice and protect the weak. Some have suggested I should be worried because this information might fall into the wrong hands. I do not feel this is going to happen. The time it takes to master this deadly art is too long for the undisciplined. Conditioning alone takes years, and mastering the striking skills takes even longer. No, I do not have to worry about some mugger possessing this skill. Anyone who takes the time and effort to reach the level of iron palm mastery will have become a much better person for the experience. If anything, I expect to find someone with the iron palm coming to my aid if I ever need help.

Learn to Hit Without the Hurt

The black belt showed me his knuckles: calloused, scarred, terribly enlarged and deformed. They drew attention to his hands. One would not think of these hands as those of a gentleman; they looked too much like those of a fighter, a martial artist to be more exact. "This was totally unnecessary," he said. "I wish someone had talked some sense into me when I was first starting out in my training years ago. If I had only known then what I know now, I would never have done this to my hands."

When you condition your hands like most martial artists, you may be taught to use methods that will leave you with hands that cannot be easily hidden from view, and will be as embarrassing as a tattoo. Ask yourself this: If someone asked you to tattoo bright red circles on the first two knuckles of each fist, with each circle to be the size of a quarter, would you? If you did, your hands would forever draw attention to themselves, and people would be constantly asking what was wrong. There is more, however, to the reason for not doing this to your hands than just appearance. The damage that many martial artists inflict on their knuckles for the sake of a powerful fist is absolutely unnecessary. I know there are many who do not feel powerful unless they have knuckles that can go through boards and bricks, but there are other parts of the hands that will do the same thing and not become deformed in the process. One must remember that those powerful fists are only the beginning of martial arts skills, not a complete system unto itself. Without advanced theory, they are nothing more than two blind dragons.

In the December, 1985 issue (**Vol. 12, No. 12**) of *Inside Kung-Fu*, I outlined a method of conditioning with dit da jow for the hands. It is a method that has been handed down through the centuries, and I have used it with great success. My hands are not scarred, nor are they inflexible, yet I am capable of breaking boards and bricks.

Why did that man say to me that he would have done things differently had he known then what he knew now? One of the reasons was the obvious embarrassment he had suffered over the years by hands that did not look normal; but another reason was that he discovered he was a blind man being led by another blind man. He had followed an ancient hand conditioning process that had been given to him by someone who never questioned the senselessness of it, and he was told not to question it. It was, "Accept this ancient tradition handed down to us from men of old who were very wise." No one ever said, "If times have changed, some of this knowledge may need to be modified to fit the circumstances." That would be considered sacrilege, an insult to those of old who could never make a mistake. The older something is, the more people tend to venerate it, which really makes no sense at all. Write something on a piece of paper, add several hundred years, and it becomes too sacred to challenge. Yet, consider this: How they treated the flu in A.D. 1400 and how it is treated today are two totally different methods, the latter being based on modification because of better knowledge developed with time. This same principle must be applied here, and changes in conditioning methods are long overdue.

Why did ancient warriors turn their hands into such deadly fighting tools? Because times were feudal. A man lived or died, quite often, because of the skill and power, or the lack thereof, in his hands. It was a decree of survival, in such warring and perilous times, that one put deadliness of hands first; appearance and medical problems that might develop later could not be of concern. However, feudal times are over, *fighting is no longer a way of life.* One does not have to eat, sleep and live fighting. Our societies are more ordered, with laws against assault and battery. A physical confrontation in today's society is rare for most of us.

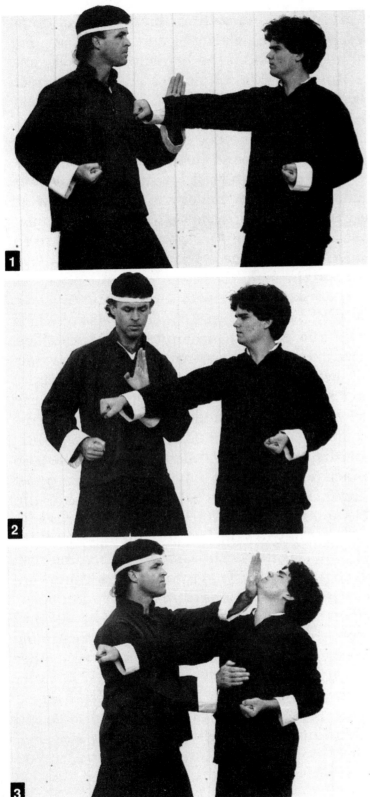

As master Gray's student throws a punch (1), Gray begins to rock back and parry with his palm. His torso also begins to turn clockwise. Once the attack has been successfully shunted away (2), Gray's circle, which is in the waist, reverses direction to counterclockwise. Gray's waist has made a figure-8, in that he started with a clockwise circle while rocking back, and ended with a counterclockwise circle as he rocked forward to attack (3).

There are those who live in areas known for high levels of crime activity, and for those who do, the knowledge of guns is a reality. For this region of terror, the gun has replaced the hardened knuckles, and the warrior who employs it usually has no moral guideline by which he lives, for, while the gun may make you deadlier, it doesn't make you better. The discipline of martial arts makes you better, and martial artists, through years of training, become better people, less prone to fight, while gunslingers, on the other hand, usually die by the same violence they produce. A gun in the hands of a martial artist is even deadlier, but when the guns run out of bullets, what then? Always remember that while the gun is a deadly weapon, it is not impossible to defeat. I have faced guns on more than one occasion in the streets, and I am still very much alive and unharmed.

Often, someone will point to mind-boggling demonstrations of someone smashing a huge stack of bricks with those bare knuckles, as if to say that those deformed knuckles are a match for a gun, which logically they are not, and a gun can turn up anywhere, at any time. One's hands no longer need be capable of piercing a warrior's armor. In any situation requiring self-defense, there are two main things to consider: the attacker's force should be redirected. The term "force" can also refer to the aim of an attacker's gun; and the attacker should be neutralized by striking a vulnerable spot on the body.

The vulnerable spots on the human body, ranging from simple pain to instant death, can be activated without having to condition the knuckles. In my second book, *Advanced Iron Palm*, I devote an entire section to these vulnerable spots. When one has learned these points and their various effects, all one has to do is concentrate enough force in one of several types of hand positions and anatomy does the rest. These hand positions, which are most effective for "spot hitting," are called "small hand techniques." These consist of "eye of the phoenix," "dragon's head," "single spearhand," "single-finger Buddah hand," and "crane's beak." They are preferred by many for spot hitting for the simple reason that they compress more pounds per square inch than other hand positions.

This brings me to *dim mak*, which is often erroneously called "delayed death touch" by those who are not trained in its use. Dim mak and *dien hsueh* are synonyms, dim mak being Cantonese dialect and dien hsueh being Mandarin dialect. Both translate into "spot hitting." If you want to talk about delayed death touch, call it *do ming dien mo*.

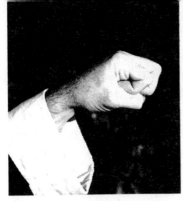
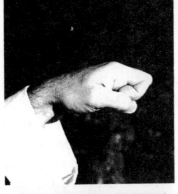

Clockwise from top left: dragon's head; eye of the phoenix; single spearhand; single-finger Buddah hand; and crane's beak.

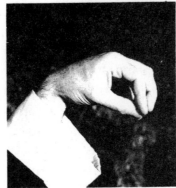

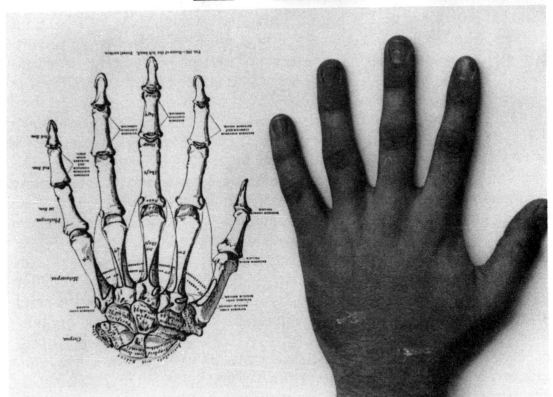

We tend to think of our hand as the way it appears on the right, when in reality, we should think of it as it would appear on the left, because with or without the skin covering, those bones are equally susceptible to damage.

When I refer to turning, or redirecting, an attacker's force, it is necessary to understand certain basic principles, the main being that it is not necessary to match force with equal force. One does not have to have bulging biceps and knuckles that look like ball-peen hammers to accomplish this redirecting of forces. Those who practice the push hands exercises of tai chi chuan will know what I mean. Consider the Spanish matador who turns the powerful bull, with its huge, deadly horns, using nothing more than a soft, flowing cape. One must develop an awareness, a sensitivity, to another's motion of direction and follow a person's intended direction of movement by physically maintaining contact with them, in most cases by touching the moving body part.

Because the knuckles are covered by skin, most people tend to overlook the damage they are doing to bones they cannot see. They strike the knuckles against every conceivable hard object to build a calloused fist. As I have said, this is unnecessary if one knows where to strike. I am showing a diagram of the bones of the hand with this chapter for the education of those who do not realize just how fragile those bones are. When you go striking and traumatizing these joints, calcium is immediately deposited around them in an enlarging process that is a one-way street. Often, arthritis follows in the years to come. Striking should be practiced only against padded objects when it comes to striking with the bony parts of the hand. Parts that are covered by muscle are the recommended anatomical parts to be used when practicing striking against solid objects. Remember, if you are in a fight only once in a year, and for most people even that is a very high average, striking with your knuckles while in that fight may not cause you any permanent damage. Therefore, the repeated, daily pounding against the knuckles to have a deadly fighting tool is not grounded in common sense. If I were in danger of being attacked by fist fighters each day, and if I could guarantee that at least once a day I would have to physically be involved in a fight, and if there were no guns in existence, then I might justify hardening my hands in the old-fashioned ways, but look at all the "ifs." We are living in a different time, and that type of abuse of the hands is no longer necessary.

In all of 1988, I was only attacked three times, partly because I stay out of areas that are known to be trouble. Two of the attacks were by people without weapons, and in one instance I was even outnumbered five-to-one. In both of the unarmed attacks, I dissuaded the attackers from getting physical, and diffused the event with no violence. The third event was when two gunmen tried to hold me up late at night. One of them made the mistake of putting a gun in my ribs, and he will never forget the lesson I taught him that night. However, in all three instances I never used my knuckles, which I hope illustrates what I have been saying. The use of the knuckles for striking is so seldom required, that disfigurement and its related problems are unnecessary for today's martial artist.

Iron Palm Training

S tanding like a strange stone monument, the stack of smooth, gray bricks reflects not only the day's light but my thoughts as well. I am amazed that anyone would even attempt to do this. "It's impossible," I tell myself, yet, as the skeletal old man places his outstretched palm on the topmost block, I cannot avert my eyes.

Instantly the gaze on the old man's face changes from a look of imperturbable calm to an intense stare. Like a wave breaking on some shore, a motion travels down his arm and into his now lifted palm. A sound like a slap rings out and a lightning crack appears down the stack of blocks. With no spacers between them, 12 stone bricks crumble into dust.

The words "iron palm" conjure up images of supernatural feats performed at the hand of a select group of kung-fu men known as the "iron palm masters." Men whose hands crush solid objects with effortless movement. Minus those individuals who press fraudulent claims, this is an accurate picture strange as it may seem. For the true iron palm is not only powerful and deadly, but the high levels of achievement reached by true practitioners produces a palm that appears to move softly, yet hits with the force of tons. There are those who before and after this chapter will not hesitate to lay claim to this deadly skill, but when called upon to demonstrate, they are capable of only the most rudimentry of strikes performed with external power and cheap, craftily arranged props.

In this sequence, a palm block is performed with the right hand (left) and followed by a left palm strike over the heart. A qualified strike to this area can lead to cardiac arrest, once again if delivered by an iron palm master. The iron palm practitioner practices his art by breaking. The ability of the practitioner to break indicates his mastery to use the technique in a self-defense situation.

At this point I should point out what the iron palm is—and what the iron palm is not. Only after three years of patient conditioning through a step-by-step process is the hand even ready to be described as an iron palm. However this alone is not a guarantee of anything except a very strong, non-bruisable hand. Training could end at this point by a student being dismissed from the school, and the student would not be capable of performing any of the spectacular feats associated with the iron palm. Conditioning is, therefore, only a first step, and continues after the three-year period, although to a less rigorous schedule.

Conditioning and Training

Using one of several recipes, a concoction of herbs is put into the skin, and the palm is toughened by striking with different hand and finger positions into a container filled with a variety of striking materials. In some methods the container is heated, producing a cooked palm which is reddened and ugly in appearance—a dead giveaway that the person is a practitioner. In the method I use, the material is kept at room temperature, and no damage to the skin's appearance results. This is the more prized method as it affords secrecy in public, with no one knowing that one is an iron palm practitioner unless the skill is

Here, the left hand executes a wrist control block (left), and then, maintaining wrist control, the back of the palm is applied to the side of the neck (right). The proper strike force in this situation can result in disrupted blood flow to the brain when performed by a master.

demonstrated, or individuals are told in secret. In any case, the palm once conditioned, is quite strong.

If one sees the iron palm training method and attempts to duplicate it without seeking training from a qualified practitioner, improper training can result in a weakening of the heart and even heart attack. At my kung-fu temple, no one, be he student or visitor, is allowed to watch training. For the reason of health, as well as keeping ancient secrets from unscrupulous individuals, this rule is strictly enforced.

After conditioning has produced the desired palm, theory of breaking is introduced to the student. It is at this point that the practitioner truly begins his study, the refinement of which will continue to his dying day. Improvement is continuous, starting from simple breaks on one block and increasing to multiple stacks.

In the practice of iron palm, breaking is serious business. It helps to judge whether or not one's techniques are powerful enough to be effectively applied in a self-defense situation. Those saying that boards and bricks do not fight back are merely reciting an old cliché used as a retort against those who equate brick and board breaking with powerful fighters. The cliché does not apply here, and any who use it have no understanding of the value and place breaking holds for the devotee of the iron palm.

Breaking with the Iron Palm

As any cheating robs the practitioner of advanced skill, one *never* indulges in the use of spacers between the blocks, meaning you have only to break the first block, momentum breaks the rest. Remove the spacers and any "master" who has been impressing gullible laymen will be stopped, unable to perform his break. Also, soft blocks such as cinder and sandblocks are *not* used. There is an integrity here to be maintained, and maintained for one reason: it is the only method that will graduate the student to the awesome level of proficiency possessed by true masters of the art.

As the student continues his study of breaking, he learns to break in unusual ways. After learning to break one-inch, two-inch, then three-inch blocks, and so on, the student begins to learn how to project his force beyond the palm's point of contact. This enables one to strike an enemy's armor and penetrate the body without having to remove the armor. The student at this point is taught how to place one block on top of another, slap the top block, and break only the bottom block without damaging the top block in any way. When the student has accomplished this, he is taught more selective skills such as long-distance transference. By placing sheets of paper between the palm and block, the palm's power must travel completely through the paper to the block, breaking it. Starting with only a few inches of paper, progression grows to stacks over two feet thick.

One might wonder how controlled a skilled palm can be. One master I know can take a stack of blocks, drop his palm, and break selectively, any block in the stack you pick, leaving all the others on either side of the block completely unbroken. He can also reverse the action, breaking everything on either side of the chosen block and leaving the chosen block still untouched.

The late Ku Yu Cheong, the most famous iron palm master of this century, once killed a horse with his palm when he thought the horse was going to trample one of his students. He slapped the large Russian workhorse on the back, whereupon the horse dropped and expired on the spot. An autopsy of the horse revealed that the organs directly beneath the spinal area struck by Cheong's palm were severly bruised and ruptured.

Suffice it to say that the iron palm is deadly. It takes years to achieve this skill, and few know its secrets. Those who do, guard such knowledge

58

with their lives. I have been asked by martial artists—as well as laymen—to teach this skill. Many made the request with a casual attitude, as if they expected me to say yes. They did not understand what they were asking. The real seeker willing to study this, my art, will wait patiently until he is asked to begin his study. It is a necessary appendage to the skills I teach. Once a student knows form, he must add power, and one technique of power is the iron palm. The skill is a necessary point in the transition from student to master. Those who ask for the skill of the iron palm merely to entertain or awe an audience lose the value of it, and their requests are always rejected.

Seeing how long and difficult the training is, and how difficult it is to find a master who will train one in secret, it is a wonder that people so casually state that they possess the iron palm, or call their breaking demonstrations by the same name. Just because one can break using his fist or palm does not mean that the person has mastered the iron palm.

The iron palm is exactly what the name states; it is not a knife hand, hammerfist, nor any other familiar hand technique. It is just a palm—but a palm that is as strong as iron.

CHAPTER EIGHT

Iron Palm Conditioning Method

There is a centuries-old feeling in kung-fu circles that the method of conditioning the hand in iron palm training should remain a closely guarded secret. In days gone by that feeling was understandable, in part to keep the procedure from falling in the hands of enemies or individuals who would misuse it. Today such a feeling is a combination of tradition and jealousy; kung-fu people did not want karate people knowing this ancient kung-fu skill. But times change. Whether a man's hands are scarred or unmarked does nothing to change or explain the nature of his heart. Therefore, for those sincere martial artists who wish to avoid the unnecessary disfigurement of their hands, I offer the following:

DO NOT:
1. Punch a *makiwara* with the knuckles until the knuckles are enlarged;
2. Do knuckle push-ups on sandpaper or other porous surfaces to build up callouses;
3. Spear the hand into buckets filled with sand;
4. Break boards or bricks with the knuckles of the fist.

INSTEAD
1. Use the knife-edged hand, hammerfist, palm heel or flat palm;
2. Use the method for conditioning the hand known as the Shaolin Temple Iron Hand Palm Conditioning Method.

Shaolin Temple Iron Palm Conditioning Method

This is regarded as the superior form of hand conditioning, as it strengthens muscles, skin, and bones—yet leaves no scars, bruises, or deformities.

Place in an urn—or wok—enough dried peas to fill it to a depth of six or more inches. With the urn on a waist-high pedestal, stand in a horse stance and drop the hand into the peas from shoulder height. Drop the hand 10-to-20 times with the shoulder relaxed so that the shock of impact does not travel to the heart. If the strike is executed too tensely the heart suffers. The hand should be dropped with the striking surfaces being the palm, the back of the palm, and the knife-edge. Do not strike the fingertips—this weakens the eyes. Instead, use a raking motion.

Before *and* after each session, apply a liberal amount of the Chinese liniment called *dit da jow* to the hands. Without the liniment, scarring is inevitable. After no less than 10, but not more than 20 strikes with each hand, stand upright and shake the hand vigorously for a few seconds for circulation, and flex the muscles in the hand by using isometrics such as the chi kung series which opens and closes the fist. Push out, then draw back, so that the whole arm is worked for circulation. Complete this set after each set of right and left strikes.

Following the workout, do not eat and do not wash the hand for one hour. Perform this workout as often as possible. In the Shaolin Temple it was practiced three times daily: once in the morning, again at noon, and a final time in the evening. To attain the traditional iron palm, one must perform this conditioning exercise three times a day for a period of three years. After three years it is only necessary to do it once a week.

After six months, change the peas to an equal mixture of dried peas and stone pebbles. Continue conditioning with this mixture for six more months, completing the first year of training. After passing this mark discard the dried peas and continue the conditioning exercise using only stone pebbles. After six months of this, substitute an equal amount of stone pebbles *and* iron pellets. The pellets must be of iron, no other metal, and care should be taken to insure that there are *no* cuts on the hands during conditioning. At the two-year mark, discard the pebbles and perform the conditioning exercise using only the iron pellets. Continue until the third year of conditioning is completed. The condition of the iron palm has been reached; conditioning is now done but once

a day and eventually but once a week. With the completion of the regimen the practitioner will have a hand that can shatter bricks and boards without injury or scarring.

This secret has been guarded for centuries, being handed down to only a select few within time-honored tradition. It is not easy to break with such a tradition, but having seen the scarred and disfigured hands of those who have been misinformed as to the conditioning procedure, I am prompted to break my silence. For this reason, I part with tradition to share a portion of the iron palm knowledge in the hope that it will prevent other martial artists, regardless of style, from experiencing irreversible damage.

Tibet: World of the Supernatural

Is there a world between heaven and earth, a world which operates under a different set of laws of physics? Are there godlike powers held by a chosen few who tread a path that lies very close to the life beyond? How close can one come to the death threshold and still live? How deeply into life can one delve and still enjoy the knowledge brought from the other side of death, from life beyond what we consider reality? These questions are difficult to answer; there are those who, after reading this article, will rush to seek things they are not spiritually prepared to encounter. However, so much improper information is being written about the arts of Tibet, the subject of supernatural claims must be addressed.

To answer the questions I have posed, we must understand the subject through three factors: life in Tibet before 1959, the takeover of

This is a woodcut of the famous Huan-To, a Buddhist priest who symbolizes the pain and suffering of the people of Tibet since the Communist takeover.

Tibet by the Communist Chinese, and the current government of Tibet in exile.

Before 1959

In Tibet, the elevation is the highest in the world. Thus, the temperatures are among the coldest. Subsequently, life is very different. Few know how to swim and dead citizens are not buried. The bodies of the deceased are taken by the "body breakers" into the mountains, broken into pieces and fed to the vultures. Many things those of another country might consider among life's necessities may be unknown in this kingdom on the "rooftop of the world." Sparse living conditions, harsh winters and yak dung burned for heat are merely the beginning.

A common practice is to immerse a newborn baby into the freezing waters of a nearby stream. If it dies, it was not meant to live in this unforgiving land; if it lives, it will become a member of a kingdom whose people do not want to know about the rest of the world, and equally refuse to allow outsiders past their borders. This is Shangri-la, Tibet before 1959.

Buddhism is its predominant religion, and while there are several sects of Buddhists here, as well as a few Moslems, they live together harmoniously, recognizing as their one king the living incarnation of the God of Mercy, Chenresi. They call him the Dalai Lama, or Great Ocean. He is considered to have lived 13 lives prior to this, his 14th, as the ruler, the dalai, and each life was selflessly devoted to his people. He has said, however, that this may be his last visit to this earthly plane, and one cannot begin to imagine how this saddens the Tibetans. He is their hope.

The Dalai Lama is so revered that when he went to India in 1950, his entourage of armor bearers, guards, valets and pathmarkers stretched five miles long. Wherever his chair passed, the ground was marked as holy. No one was allowed to set foot on the land. So revered, that on March 10, 1959, when the Chinese sought to capture him at his palace in Lhasa, Tibetans numbering in the thousands used their bodies to block the gates leading into Potala. They would rather die than see their God-king being taken from them. They also failed to budge as the Chinese Army slaughtered untold numbers of Tibetan men, women and children who stood in its way. Nonetheless, the Dalai Lama had been secretly removed from the Potala the night before and was being hastily taken to safety in India.

One child out of every family is given to become a monk. The child is usually around five. Training in the many arts of discipline, he will live the rest of his life in a monastery. Rising at night to pray, in the morning hours to pray and at sunrise to pray, he will spend what little time he has left doing the temple chores, memorizing the scriptures and studying the arts he has chosen to protect. The food eaten by the monks is spartan to say the least—cracked barley mixed with butter, and strong tea. Always the same thing, no change, nothing to distract the mind. Is it a key, perhaps, to finding powers of the mind?

There are different teachers for different arts, but all are taught to protect their various arts. They are guarded so well, in fact, the teachers will deny the existence of certain phenomena when queried by laymen. The denial not only skirts the issue, but is so cleverly worded the questioner leaves thinking his question has been answered. Much later, however, he realizes he has been tricked.

Could it be the price to discover these secrets is to walk to the very window of death and see the other side, and having once viewed the plane beyond, to return with an alternate view of this level of existence and its reasons?

This is a price too steep for most, yet the lama of Tibet practice a form of traveling beyond the limits of death through out-of-body training to learn their secrets. There is a practice they call "seclusion," which is certain death for anyone but the chosen. When a monk has reached a fixed level of discipline, he will obtain permission from the abbot of his monastery to enter seclusion. He will then enter a chamber carved into the side of a mountain. The size of the chamber is 12 feet by 12 feet by eight feet. The room is bare; no chair, no bed, no light, no noise. The door is sealed from the outside. Every two days, a bowl of food and water will be passed to the monk via a passageway that permits no noise, conversation or light to enter his self-imposed prison. One soon loses all sense of time, and for those truly unprepared, the loss of sanity may follow. The result is a horrible death brought on by fear. How long the monk remains in his chamber is up to the individual, but the minimum is one year! Some will stay two, five, even ten or 20 years, while others will leave seclusion only to return. What happens in there??

During his stay, the monk will strive for out-of-body experiences from which he will return with everything from new chants for the other monks, many of whom can hum three notes at the same time, to more knowledge of seemingly supernatural acts. Some never return

68

to this plane of existence and die a peaceful death in seclusion. The return from this walk through the valley of the shadow of death creates a monk who defies description. One can see why they do not perform their feats for the simple entertainment of bystanders. However, there have been occasions when the uninitiated Westerner has accidentally observed the forbidden. One person so fortunate was female explorer Alexandra David-Neel.

Having spent several years in Tibet at the beginning of this century, she witnessed the art of lightness, called *lung gom*, one day in the northern part of the country. In her diary she wrote that she saw a speck moving across the plain with such speed, she at first thought it was an antelope. But when she raised her field glasses to get a better look, she was startled to find the object was a man — a lama to be exact. She asked her guides is she could interview and photograph him. But they said no.

"You must not stop the lama," they said, "or even speak to him, as it would surely kill him. The lama must not break their meditation or the god who is in them will escape if they cease repeating the chant or special meditation prayer. If the god leaves them before the proper time, he shakes them so hard that they die."

Another time, while in western Tibet, David-Neel came upon a lama who was sitting on some rocks. Deep in meditation, he was naked except for iron chains wrapped around his body. For some time he was unaware of her presence.

"Suddenly," she noted, "he sprang like a deer, chains and all and was gone." She was told later, "They wear the chains to make themselves heavy since lung gom makes their bodies so light they are in danger of floating off into the air." It should be noted that in ancient kung-fu texts, there are stories of these arts from the Chinese who bordered Tibet.

The Fall of Tibet

In 1950, the Communists invaded Tibet, saying their intentions were honorable. The Dalai Lama worked patiently with the government of Peking to restore freedom and peace to his troubled country, but in 1959, the Chinese tried to murder him. On the evening of March 9, his holiness was secretly removed from the Potala and taken by his guardians to India where, in Dharmsala, he set up his government in exile. A day later, thinking the Dalai Lama was still in his place, the Communists opened fire and began a very destructive country-wide campaign, which included destroying monasteries and holy places, murdering priests and lama, burning sacred books, and committing genocide. The great temples of Sera, Drepung and Gaden, once housing thousands, now lay silent. Many Tibetans fled the holocaust by crossing the mountain passes into India. The snows were so bright that those fleeing had to wrap their hair braids around their eyes to keep from going blind. In some places, the snow was so deep that many described surviving only by walking on the "roads" created by bones of those who did not make it.

The horrors awaiting them in Tibet made them determined to escape. In one village, 22 parents were executed as an example to the rest. Their crime: refusing to send their children to the new Communist school. The method of execution: spikes driven through the eyes. Live burials were common, and these horrors have driven 150,000 from their homes, and more than one million to their deaths. There are only six million Tibetans left as the Communist genocide continues.

Some of the sacred books made it to Dharmsala. Some of the "walking books," the lama who memorized entire texts, also escaped and are now recreating a temporary Tibet in the mountains of India. They all await the day they can return to their beloved country. The sacred arts of Tibet have a price that cannot be bought with silver or gold. Supernatural feats and staggering powers of the mind do exist. Some examples would make this article sound like a collection of fairy tales. There is indeed a world at the other end of the spectrum of experiences. It is measured by a different clock and ruled by an alien passion. Witness the words from "The Mountain:"

You have asked me to tell you about the mountain. Some of you have even begged me to tell you about the mountain. Whether you ask or beg, I will not tell you, but if you truly ask I will try to tell you.

If I tell you about the mountain, you will not see it. If I take you to see it, you will not hear what I have to say.

If, as I tell you about the mountain, I tell you about the trees that grow on its banks, the beautiful trees that seem to grow forever in awesome oneness with the sky, and you suddenly say, "Ah! I know now what the mountain looks like," you will go and teach trees, and those whom you teach will not see the mountain for the trees.

If, as I tell you about the mountain, I tell you about the beautiful streams that cascade down its side, streams that seem to carry the conversations of the sages on their rushing tongues, and you suddenly say, "Ah! I know now what the mountain looks like," you will go and teach streams, and those whom you teach will build rafts.

If, as I tell you about the mountain, I tell you about the caves I discovered while climbing its heights, the deep caves filled with wonderful silence and solemnity, and you suddenly say, "Ah! I know now what the mountain looks like," you will go and teach caves, and those whom you teach will dig holes and become old men.

If, as I tell you about the mountain, I tell you about the mountain's peak, how it scrapes the sky with god-like power for all its towering splendor, yet is at one with all around it, and you suddenly say, "Ah! I know now what the mountain looks like," you will go and teach mountain tops, and those whom you teach will call themselves teachers.

If you truly ask me to tell you, I will tell you where I went and how; I will point the way, but I will not be your hands and feet. If you ask me how fast I ran to find the mountain, I will not tell you. If you truly ask me where the mountain may be found, I will point to the path. If you ask me how hard it was to climb, my ears will hear the conversation of ants with the deer, and the songs of butterfly wings. If you hear these things, you have been to the mountain.

Some blind themselves, while some blind others, and there are even those who blind themselves while blinding others. They blind by demanding to be recognized as part of the mountain, but when they have gone, the trees will grow on, the caves will solemnize for centuries to come, the streams will speak wisdom, and the mountain's peak will still draw a line between heaven and earth. I have been to the mountain and found I could not speak, I could only point and hear.

CHAPTER TEN

The Iron Palm—
What You Need
to Know

Iron Palm Injuries

There are no kung-fu schools in Kansas to my knowledge. Because of many injuries—broken bones, a knee injury and lower back injury—I've been out of class more than in. Three of the bones broken have been in my hands from sparring or competing. Two in my left hand and one in my right hand. The last was on December 5, 1985, and I've been out of class since trying to decide whether or not to continue.

Would you please answer some questions for me?

First of all, I missed the article you wrote for *Inside Kung-Fu* magazine and only found out about you through the letters people wrote in later issues. I've heard some negative things about iron palm training. Please set me straight. First I heard that if not done properly under direct supervision, you could develop blood clots or arthritis, or become ill with internal problems. Also I read in a book that you cannot just quit in the middle. That you need a special diet to follow while training and there are periods you must abstain from sex and alcohol. It also stated that iron palm is a negative kung and that you could not hold a child in your hands too long because you would draw life from it. Brian, are these things true?

I wanted to learn iron palm to harden my hands to so that I could study the martial arts without any more injuries to my hands and not have to be put in a cast by the doctor every time I try and fulfill my dream. I *don't* want to quit now and be one of the thousands who begin training and never see it through. Please understand and help me.

Emidio Gomez
El Dorado, KS

Before answering your questions, I must comment on what you have been doing to your hands. When any martial artist damages and disfigures his hands while trying to either learn breaking or train in the art of his choosing, he is doing something wrong. Disfigurement of the body went out with feudal times. In those days it was often necessary to condition body parts to be able to use them as weapons when weapons were not available, because one's life literally depended from day to day on survival skills.

For some reason, I suppose because of a lack of historical education and plain old common sense, many of the ancient and outmoded methods of hand conditioning were kept alive. Such things as beating the hands against stones and thrusting them into buckets of sand obviously lead to hands that are scarred, coarse, reddened, and, sometimes inflexible. However, this is not the only way to destroy them. Training improperly can also do it. While training under feudal methods is, as far as I am concerned, training improperly, I am referring to two ways in which a person can be training improperly (i.e., being self-taught, or training under someone who does not know what he is doing). That may sound oversimplified, but in the majority of cases I have seen in my years of training, these have been the reasons.

Breaking solid objects is not merely yelling, hitting as hard as you can and blocking out the pain. It is a very involved science. Many self-taught practitioners have gone around the country putting on phony demonstrations and have built big names and reputations on skills that would not stand up to close scrutiny. When you see them putting spacers between the materials that they are going to break, or scoring the ice in those so-called "awesome" ice-breaking demos, know that their skills have been handed down from the self-taught lineage.

If your broken bones are from sparring, again, if it is a common occurrence, something is wrong. In my school, I often have people sign up for study, and they are ready to tell me how they are going to train. If they are not going to get to spar right away, and spar every night, then they are ready to go elsewhere. I always ask people with this type of mentality, "If you are going to spar, what are you going to spar with?" The answer, of course, is form, and one they hate to admit to, for it means work. One has to learn basic forms and progress on to more advanced forms, and these forms should contain all of the self-defense techniques and fight theories utilized in their particular system or style. As you have grown up, you have acquired instinctive reactions, reactions that you would

74

respond with when attacked. When the forms that you are training in become your instinctive response, then you are truly ready to spar as you finally have something to spar with. If you are being forced to spar too soon, and you are forced to spar with someone who has neither the proper attitude nor the skill of control, then you are opening yourself up to injury, and the teacher who forces you into this type of situation is not very well-trained.

Now to answer your questions about the iron palm. It is true that a person can develop problems from not training properly in the iron palm conditioning and in the application. As for developing blood clots and arthritis, while this may be a possibility, it is hard to do; yet there are problems with striking that can lead to weakening of the heart, and even heart attack. If one is not taught to keep the arm relaxed while striking the conditioning materials, the response is sent back to the heart, continually weakening it until the problem is corrected. If a student is following my instructions carefully as they were presented in the December, 1985 issue of IKF, there should be no problem.

As for a special diet to follow, there is no scientific data that I can quote for or against a special diet. Ancient dietary prescriptions were commonplace centuries ago, but many were really unnecessary. Bear in mind that there are certain herbal concoctions taken internally or externally by some iron palm practitioners that make their hands very dangerous, even to themselves. For this reason, they must take an internal antidote daily which you might call a special diet, but beyond this, your diet is really up to you. The reason the prescriptions against alcohol and sex came down through the years is that it was felt that they reduced your body's ability to maximize the benefits of the training. Sex may reduce your energy levels for a short period after participation, but alcohol truly does interfere with your progress. First of all, let me say that true warriors never get drunk. They are always alert and would never allow themselves to be so vulnerable. Second, the liver is like the gas pedal to all of the internal organs, and when it is bogged down with the task of detoxifying your alcoholic consumption, then internal organs have their rate of productivity affected.

When some refer to the iron palm as a negative kung, they mean that its practice gives the hand a quality that does not produce health, or healthy effects, either in the practitioner or in those with whom he comes into contact with. There is, for example, a palm that excretes a poison which is due to the ingestion of a formula of secret herbs. If the owner of that palm strikes you, you will die from the contact with that poisonous excretion. What keeps that practitioner from dying from the poison is an antidote which he must take for as long as he keeps the palm "charged." Thus, holding a baby in his hands would not be

advisable, yet not every palm in the iron palm family of conditioning methods is so negative. There are over 100 secret recipes for concoctions to put in the palm, many quite harmless. The method I described in the December, 1985 IKF *is safe for everyone.*

— Brian Gray

Do You Need an Instructor?

Your article on iron palm pointed out several things I'm doing wrong, such as training fingertips, knuckle strikes, and I was using hard strikes and tensing my arms. Also my workouts were only once a day instead of three times a day and I was using dit da jow only after striking, not before and after. Someone told me once to massage the hands under hot water after striking the sandbags to spread out bruised blood. What is your opinion on this? You said not to wash the hands for one hour after a workout.

Your article also says, "If one sees the iron-palm training method and attempts to duplicate it without seeking training from a qualified practitioner, improper training can result in a weakening of the heart and even heart attack."

I have been searching for a teacher of iron palm for almost a year now and still have found no one who will personally teach me this art. I hesitate to continue to try and train on my own with only partial information. I've made many mistakes already and am trying to create healthy hands and body to stay injury free. I want no more broken bones! What I've read from you tells me I could do myself more harm than good. Isn't following a written program or even a video the same as what you were saying about attempting to duplicate the training method?

Is it acceptable to use a canvas bag filled with sand set on a bench? Is steel shot okay for later stages of training or must it be only iron pellets? If peas and stone pebbles must be used, can they be made into a bag or do they have to be loose in a container? What size of pebbles and where can I find them? If a person would get sick with the flu or something should he train anyway? Are there any conditions when a person should lay off training or must it be every day, three times a day non-stop for three years? I only want to get as much information as possible! Thank you for being patient! Can you describe the chi kung hand exercises?

There is one other thing I'd like to ask you. There are many styles of kung-fu and different people created the different styles, so how can there be iron palm as an art in several separate styles? I would think someone invented it or created it and would keep it only in his system.

Emidio Gomez
El Dorado, KS

I do not wish to mislead readers into thinking it is impossible to learn the iron palm without having an iron palm master right there with them. When I said that attempting to duplicate it without seeking training from a qualified practitioner could result in a weakening of the heart, and even heart attack, I was thinking of two examples. One case in point, a man trying to steal the art by watching, but never questioning, died of a heart attack. In the other case, a gentleman in the martial arts came to me at a tournament in Washington, D.C., and told me how he and his wife secretly filmed me in 1975 while I was giving a public demonstration of the iron palm. He had been analyzing that film and trying to learn all my secrets all those years, yet not once had he ever thought of asking me to teach him. How sad, because his hands were unnecessarily scarred from improper training. Needless to say, I recognized in him a sincere and dedicated martial artist and told him what he needed to do to train correctly.

Concerning training with a sandbag, or a bag filled with steel pellets, etc., it is really necessary for the hand to come in contact with the material you are striking. When you are striking the loose peas, pebbles or iron pellets, the material is going to form around the hand and its shape, giving you an overall conditioning, whereas, striking a closed bag is only going to hit the raised surfaces of the hand. Also, when you reach the advanced stage of using iron, the iron is actually mixing with your skin and must come into contact with it. The size of the pebbles should be about the size of peas to maximize the skin area contact. Many people ask about laying off training, and I will tell you very honestly that if a person is doing it three times a day, then taking off on Saturday and Sunday, it will not hurt, but if you are sick, your life force is down and it is not a good time to train. Also, do not train with cuts or open wounds. The iron can get into the wound and cause infection, and some herbal liniments are poisonous and kill you if they get in your blood. If you are not sure about the liniment you are using, it is a good rule of thumb not to let it get into a cut. You can make sure of what you have by asking your Oriental herbalist if the liniment can be taken internally, and if he says yes, you have no worries.

You have discovered that the recipe for dit da jow is an ancient secret, and though the recipe varies a little from kung-fu master to kung-fu master, it is true that no one will tell you what is in it. Let me be the first master, then, to ever put in print the recipe for one of the best recipes from ancient China for making dit da jow. One part each of pu huang, hsueh jin, mei yao, hung hua, and lu shiang added to four-fifths part tien ch'i, one-and-one-fifth part tse yao, and one-and-one-half parts of dang gwei and guang ch'un. Let these soak in rice wine for one year and you will have one the most potent forms of dit da jow, or you can continue to save yourself the trouble of making it and buy the best aged dit da jow in Chinatown.

When you are asking about why the iron palm isn't just known to one kung-fu style or family system, the answer is found in the history of ancient China. About 5,000 years ago, during the time in China known as the Three Legendary Heroes, Emperors Huang T'i, Shen Neng and Fu Hsi compiled and dispensed all of the herbal knowledge. The knowledge they gained through searching out all of the known herbal remedies was taught to the people throughout China to help the people better themselves. Thus, the herbal remedies used for removing bruises and promoting healing got into the mainstream of those who practiced the fighting arts as early as 2852 B.C., when the first recorded use of kung-fu is found in China. From that time, feudal China unfolded, and the knowledge of medicine evolved along with its uses. Not many know in this country that the man considered to be the father of medicine in China, Hua T'o (A.D. 150-229), was performing brain surgery, invented anesthesia and made tooth fillings centuries ahead of the West.

By 100 B.C., the art of Go Ti, the forerunner of Japanese jiujitsu, was already a national sport, and many families and schools prized their skills and secrets. Centuries of further refining martial knowledge took place at the various Shaolin Temples where, particularly at the one in Hunan province and the second most famous one in Fukien, it is felt kung-fu reached its apex. So one can understand why there are various types of iron palm methods that have come to us from China.

It is not, therefore, indigenous to any particular style. Whether or not a person knows the secrets of the iron palm depends solely on whether or not there was someone to pass it on.

— B.G.

Iron Palm Exercises

What specific exercises should I do to get ready for practicing the art of iron palm?

John Migals
Fontana, CA

Would it be possible to receive some more information from you concerning the iron palm?

Beat Maritz
Olten, Switzerland

Could you please tell me if there are any instructors of iron palm kung-fu living in England?

Mark Rowden
London, England

There are no specific exercises to do to get ready to train in the iron palm. As long as one is physically fit and does not have a bad heart, people of all sizes and shapes can train. Quite often people will write to me and ask if I can give them some more information on the iron palm. I always give them specific answers.

As you read my articles, I think you can see there is just too much information on the subject to give a seminar to each of the hundreds who write, and yet, over and over I get this request: "Would you please send me any information you have on the iron palm." First of all, there are only a handful of us in the world, and because of the immense secrecy surrounding the art, few of us know each other. I hope this changes as it is the sole reason I went public with the knowledge. I would like to see people surpass even my skills. I want to see the things that people are going to accomplish with the knowledge. I then will be able to enjoy the benefits of those unlimited by the barriers that may hold me.

— B.G.

Are There Mental Benefits?

Unfortunately, in Lebanon, there are no authentic kung-fu teachers, especially iron palm practitioners. So I preferred to ask you some questions to help me in my martial studies. What are the mental benefits of iron-palm training? What is the difference between the iron palm conditioning and the iron sand palm conditioning? It has been said that internal kung-fu training gives Shaolin monks awesome destructive power generated by small movements. Does that destructive power have something to do with the iron palm training? What are the conditions needed to be accepted as a student of the iron palm? What are its characteristics? Where is your temple located? I am six feet tall and thin. What kung-fu style is suitable for me? Recently, I bought a makiwara. Can it help me in toughening my hands without callousing or deforming them and bruising the bones? Finally, I understood from your article that kung-fu teaches humility, simplicity and honesty.

Abou Jneid Adel
Beirut, Lebanon

The mental benefits of training in the iron palm are not as great as the benefits that one gains from studying a complete art. You see, the iron palm is only a slice of a whole pie. If I take one slice of pie and call it the whole pie, I am wrong. Likewise, kung-fu is the total man. I cannot take one aspect, or portion, of my training and say it will give the mental benefits. Mental benefits come from all of the aspects combined and in their proper proportions. When we think of the awesome destructive power that the Shaolin monks were capable of generating in small movements, we cannot simply attribute this to one "secret" technique.

One technique, however, is to think of a wave that originates in the toes and moves up the legs to the hips where it is amplified and sent on to the upper torso and, finally, out the hands. Thus, the hand has the appearance of striking with a small movement, yet the kinetic energy available upon impact is staggering. Quite naturally, this method is employed in the iron palm training.

There are conditions set by most of the masters of the iron palm that must be set before they will teach anyone their skill. As I stated earlier, I have given many of the secrets of the art to the readers of Inside Kung-Fu *so that the art might be brought back from near extinction, yet there is still much that even I will not teach to the public. My reasons are the same as those set by all of the real masters of this skill. The higher levels of this art are deadly to a point that would stagger your imagination. If I were to tell you how to reach over and touch someone with your finger and kill them, you would either find me incredible, or you would believe me, but regardless of your reaction, the truth would remain. The truth is, I know how this is done, and I could teach it to you, but what remains to be seen is this: What are you going to do with this knowledge when I have given it to you? Are you going to go out and kill someone right away to see if it works? Are you going to use it for evil? Are you going to try to use it on me? We only take life when we are forced to choose between an attacker's and our own. When the master is finally convinced that you know* the value of life and have the capacity to uphold the training he demands of his students, you may be selected to carry on the knowledge. It is true that many masters take this knowledge to their graves rather than risk seeing someone die from its abuse.

Therefore, be careful of those who try to sell books and manuals on secret arts such as dim mak, spot hitting, often referred to as delayed death touch. Recently, a student brought to me a manual he had purchased which purported to teach the secrets of dim mak. It was a cheap pamphlet with black and white photos of two Chinese people demonstrating the supposed strikes, filled with impressive charts and timetables, and the results that would happen if the spots were hit in the prescribed manner. Needless to say, this book was fake, and I showed my student the reasons why, yet I could see why the average layman would be duped by it. True masters have a great respect for life.

In my years of learning kung-fu, I have been fortunate to have good frinds in the Chinese community who shared forms such as the long fist, white crane, tiger, praying mantis and the grand ultimate fist. I say fortunate, because when I was coming up, Chinese did not teach non-Chinese the art. It was unthinkable, so obtaining the little that I know was indeed a great honor. Times changed radically, thanks to the television series, "Kung Fu," which aired in the early 1970s. I know many Chinese masters, and even grandmasters, who, believe it or not, never missed a show. It did not take them long to realize that they could afford to pay their bills and buy needed extras for their schools if they cashed in on the then popular demand for kung-fu lessons. It was a good learning experience for both sides. The Chinese found that there were some Americans actually worth teaching, and the Americans learned that the art was deeper than they had at first imagined. So, years ago, it was not possible to simply ask, "What style of kung-fu is good for me?" and then simply go out and find a teacher of that style. It is not quite so easy still, but years ago your style was determined by the family you were born in, if you were Chinese, and by your luck if you weren't.

Outside China, there are still a few kung-fu schools, so you are at the mercy of fate when it comes to finding a good one. Or even finding one for that matter. Styles that I would couple with physiognomy are: crane, long fist and praying mantis for thin people: tiger for strong, quick people; ape for big, powerfully built people; choy li fut and monkey for those quick and agile who like footwork; wing chun for handwork; and tai chi for those who start late in life. There are more than 400 hundred styles of kung-fu, as different as night and day, so you have a lot to choose from.

— B.G.

84

What about the Training Routine?

The papers you have sent opened up my mind to the martial arts in a different way. I do not train at any schools or under any masters but from books mainly concerning chi. There are a lot of questions the books cannot answer and I was wondering if you have any suggestions on how I should go about getting the answers. Also, if I follow the three-year training program will it also develop me mentally as well as physically?

Richard Waters
St. Louis, MO

It is difficult finding the answers to the questions that come to us in the pursuit of martial arts. There are many who are only too willing to mislead us, and many who are unwilling to help us. I feel because of the kindness that was shown to me by those in the martial arts who cared, I am obligated to do the same and teach others likewise. Naturally, if you follow the training routine I described for the three years, you are going to develop mentally as well as physically. Making yourself do anything that long and that consistent develops a discipline that you may not have had when you first began. The endurance alone strengthens the willpower.

— B.G.

How is Chi Connected?

Can iron palm be combined with chi? How long does it take to master the skill? Are there certain techniques that iron palm can be combined with to make a good offensive/defensive art? Is it really true that you can put your hand through brick walls?

In your article, what did you mean when you said, "Don't strike with your fingers because it hurts the eyes," and "Don't tense up when striking because it hurts the heart?"

Roy Northern
Corsicana, TX

Of course the iron palm eventually has to be coupled with chi, or the advanced abilities cannot be reached. Mastery of the palm will take at least ten years. You must remember that, regardless of the charlatans running around with only three or four years of experience calling themselves master, the Shaolin masters only earned the title after spending 15-to-20 years of intensive training and testing. To borrow an old slogan, "The quality should go in before the name goes on."

Always be quick to study, slow to praise yourself. Let your good be discovered like the last rose of summer.

The iron palm can be used in any art, in any style, but there is no such thing as an offensive art, or a defensive art. There is only a correct philosophy and an incorrect philosophy. To defend what is just is honorable, to attack without right incurs a debt that is paid with time.

In my article I mentioned not striking with the fingertips. The reason is that the fingertips are referral points for the eyes, and constant pounding on them will lead to weakening of the eyes.

— B.G.

Will it Hurt My Playing?

I have practiced martial arts for seven years and I am also a guitarist-musician. I would like to know if it is possible to train and condition my hands without doing damage. Can you refer me to specific herbs used in hand conditioning? Mr. Gray, are you also aware of the meridian line that connects the fingertips and the eyes? In spearhand training do we risk sight damage?

George Masone
Massapequa, NY

Many people write to me concerning the fear of damage to their hands. I can only reiterate that following the regimen as I outlined in the December, 1985 IKF will lead to hands that are strong and unscarred. I play the piano and am known for my handwriting, which I have spent years perfecting. Neither of these skills has been affected by my training. If you ever find that you are losing any of your hand qualities, please write to me so I can find out what you are doing wrong.

— B.G.

About the Author

Master Brian Gray was born in an Army hospital at the Aberdeen Proving Grounds, Aberdeen, Md., June 22, 1951. His father, who had traveled extensively in China, often spoke of that fascinating country, and thus contributed to the interest master Gray developed for China while he was a young boy.

Before the television series "Kung Fu," finding someone Chinese who was willing to teach real kung-fu to someone who was not Chinese was next to impossible. "I was drawn to the Chinese way of life," Gray says, "since I was six years old, because my first best friend was Chinese. His mother and father were from Beijing, and through them, I met more of the people who would be influential in my martial arts training." Master Gray fit in with his Chinese friends, because he respected their traditions, learned to speak Mandarin, and treated every technique he was shown as a treasure.

Brian graduated from Academy in Erie, Pa., in 1969, and obtained a degree in language from Lee College in Cleveland, Tenn., in 1973. It was while attending Lee that Brian was first approached to teach his martial arts to several students who, as Brian puts it, "would not leave me alone." That was in 1971, and Brian has been teaching ever since. From 1981-to-1985, Brian was rated by *Karate Illustrated* magazine as one of the top five weapons champions in the Mid-Atlantic Region (Region 10). In 1986, he opened his second school in Florida (the other being in Maryland).

People are often puzzled when master Gray tells them he does not have a master. As he puts it, "The list of the Chinese who contributed to my education, while not a who's who, is lengthy. To single out any of these over another would be to belittle the contributions the others made."

Master Gray has been giving public demonstrations of his iron palm skills since 1973. He has appeared at numerous tournaments, exhibitions, and television shows both in and out of the United States. Master Gray was the first non-Chinese to demonstrate the iron palm to the American public, and has been opening the door ever wider for those eager to learn. In 1985, he published many of the details for the necessary training in *Inside Kung-Fu* magazine. The response was incredible. As a result, this book *The Complete Iron Palm,* and the soon-to-be published, *Advanced Iron Palm,* have been written.